"At the moment of my death, I want three things. I want not to be afraid. I want the people I love to know just how much I love them. . . . I want to know that I have done everything that was humanly possible to contribute to my world in some kind of way. I want to give back in gratitude for having been able to be here." —from *A Rock and a Hard Place*

"GO AHEAD, READ HIM. HE'S NOT DEPRESSING AT ALL. . . . You will see how the heart makes room to live, even in the pitch of darkness. It is for us to see if we can turn his legacy into action."
                    —Paul Monette, National Book Award
                        winner, author of *Becoming a Man*

"A riveting read and an astonishing testament to the stamina of the human spirit. From a life that has dealt him unimaginable cruelty, Tony Johnson has somehow forged an outlook rooted in compassion, good humor, and off-handed courage."
                                    —Armistead Maupin

"Reminds each of us that we must once again place our children as our first priority in life. This book is a must for every American."
                        —Marva Collins, founder,
                            Westside Preparatory School

"Very wise and thoughtful . . . Tony is very bright and exceptional, but he is also very much a 15-year-old."
                    —Amy Amabile, Executive Director
                        Northern Lights Alternatives—New York

"He is a prodigy."                    —Darryl Ponicsan

# A ROCK
# AND A
# HARD PLACE

*One Boy's Triumphant Story*

## Anthony Godby Johnson

FOREWORD BY
Paul Monette

INTRODUCTION BY
Jack L. Godby

AFTERWORD BY
Fred Rogers

A SIGNET BOOK

SIGNET
Published by the Penguin Group
Penguin Books USA Inc., 375 Hudson Street,
New York, New York 10014, U.S.A.
Penguin Books Ltd, 27 Wrights Lane,
London W8 5TZ, England
Penguin Books Australia Ltd, Ringwood,
Victoria, Australia
Penguin Books Canada Ltd, 10 Alcorn Avenue,
Toronto, Ontario, Canada M4V 3B2
Penguin Books (N.Z.) Ltd, 182–190 Wairau Road,
Auckland 10, New Zealand

Penguin Books Ltd, Registered Offices:
Harmondsworth, Middlesex, England

Published by Signet, an imprint of Dutton Signet,
a division of Penguin Books USA Inc. This is an authorized reprint
of a hardcover edition published by Crown Publishers.

First Signet Printing, June, 1994
10  9  8  7  6  5  4  3  2  1

 REGISTERED TRADEMARK—MARCA REGISTRADA

Printed in the United States of America

PUBLISHER'S NOTE
This is a true story. Certain names and descriptions have been changed to
protect the privacy of others.

*With love and respect*
*to the*
*Body Mechanic*


Thanks for 24-7, not eating all of my brownies,
and for losing so many bets to me.
I know you don't do kids but you did me, fine.
I love you.

# Acknowledgments

This book was not a singular effort. I'd like to take the time now to thank those people who stood behind me and helped and guided me:

My family. You've all been everything I ever dreamed of.

Wendy Weil, for believing in me from the very start and getting the ball rolling. It's okay that you're a Cubs fan.

David Groff, a top-notch editor who journeyed with me to release the freedom within ourselves to make the pages come alive. Without David and his sensitivity, this book could not have grown so beautiful, and neither could we.

Carol Taylor, for being "such a girl" and letting me have someone to write a poem about. We overcame!

Amalia Fuchs, for all of the late-night laughs. You are one of the brightest spots in my heart. I believe in magic, too.

Norma Godin, New Jersey executive director of the Make-A-Wish Foundation, for seeing to it

## *Acknowledgments*

that I have a computer, which made the writing of this book easy and fun.

Scott Godin, for knowing everything there is to know about computers and for being so available every time I bombed my system—not to mention for having access to great card games that came in handy when I needed a distraction.

Jean Herche, for reminding me to look for my own creativity. There will always be candles on the water.

Sally Fisher, for reminding us all that circumstances don't determine quality.

Amy Amabile, for being a good friend and supplying musical entertainment during those involved editing sessions.

# Contents

# Contents

# *Foreword*

I have not been much in the market for new
friends, not these days. I feel like I've already
buried half my address book, and the other half
is taking care of me as best it can. Doubtless I
hear more than my share of the pain of AIDS,
because so many people write to me, their isolation broken at last by a chance encounter with
something I've written. In return I scribble a line
or two when I can. I like to think I speak for
them sometimes, who are otherwise so invisible,
so unheard. But for sheer self-protection I can't
take on any more cases. I can't cure it, neither
the virus nor the grief. There is only what
guarded energy I have to finish my own time, a
last few scrawls of writing, a precious hour with
those I love.

So it was nothing out of the ordinary to open
Tony's letter, a year ago last August. To be sure,
it was the first letter I'd had from a thirteen-
year-old, remarkably poised and even witty. He
hadn't actually bought my books, he said, but
traded with a guy in the hospital for a couple of

sports magazines. He said he understood about sickness because he'd fought a long battle himself, though he spoke of it all without self-pity, and at the time he wasn't even diagnosed with AIDS. In a half-sentence here and there he'd make glancing reference to the abuse he'd suffered at the hands of his so-called blood family. But how lucky he was all the same, he was quick to assure me, to have found himself a new family who loved him. Two years of healing had finally begun to obliterate the horrors he had endured. In a word, he was happy.

I wrote him back, as much as anything to clear my desk before leaving for a trip back East. Ten days later I returned to find a message from his adoptive mother on my answering machine, thanking me, saying how much it meant to him because he'd been pretty sick lately. On a sudden impulse I called her back. And was quickly struck mute by her recitation of the details of the boy's tortured journey. I admit it, I wanted to run. I'd seen enough pain to last me one lifetime, thank you. She heard the uncertainty in my voice, the helplessness I guess, and quickly reassured me: "You don't *have* to talk to him. But you'll like him, I promise. He's not depressing at all."

She was right. It's the world that's depressing, not Tony Johnson. His voice was irrepressible, spilling over with humor, aching with life. His official AIDS diagnosis was about a month away, but I knew it in my bones from the very first. It happened that my own immune system was nose-diving at the same time, and I felt myself withdrawing. I felt that only three or four people in my life could really understand what I was on the brink of. But Tony became one of them, I think because he was so unflinchingly honest, so open about his own struggle to survive, to believe there was love out there worth fighting for.

We became a couple of moon men, talking late at night before that grate came clanking down at the bar across the street from his house. It still amazes me that I've never met him, that it's all transpired over the phone, like we're a couple of spies behind enemy lines, communicating in code. As he got sicker and sicker, battling the foe, I thought every conversation was going to be the last. And he was going to die faceless and voiceless like everyone else in the plague, to satisfy the smug superiority of those who remained untouched and in denial.

There's no good news about AIDS. It doesn't respond to cheap-shot pieties about courage and endurance, not when you get up close to it. The suffering is beyond measure. The whole landscape—moonscape, rather—is littered with land mines, new demented twists of infection, new contortions of intolerance. People with AIDS are generally blamed for being sick, and especially among some Fundamentalist Christians, AIDS itself is perceived as the cure, so why bother to cure it? Don't ever forget—we don't—that this nightmare was allowed to happen, by a government indifferent to everything but greed.

There is still not war on AIDS, no commitment to fight it except to cook the figures and lie about the funding. History will note that we sat and watched the fire burn, our faces seared with shame, because we were too afraid to talk about sex or needles. "*I'm* not going to get it," crow the masses, with the same giddy fervor with which they proclaim, "No new taxes!" Everyone's on his own.

But unlike so many, Tony Johnson would not die on his own, faceless and voiceless. After he got AIDS, Tony got himself a computer and started to write in earnest. An active kid, he wanted to stay engaged in spite of a life that was increasingly bedridden—prey to medieval medical procedures and a system that told him right to his face that he ought to be dead by now. Yet as he searched his life for something to leave behind, the words he found were anything but play. He had a grasp of the meaning of things, an urgency to make sense of it all, and a rare talent for giving life to the page. We don't really know where writers come from, or what stands the best of them apart to serve witness to more than themselves. But whatever special grace is required, Tony has it in spades.

Even so, it wasn't an easy journey. Effortless though his voice sounds in these pages, it was a voice that had to be fought for, inch by inch on the front lines. There were times when he truly despaired, couldn't see the shape of what he was making and couldn't believe he had the days or the strength to bring it off. Who cared anyway? It was in the middle of one of those spasms of doubt that I told him not to forget that the greatest human testament we have from the Second World War was written by a fourteen-year-old girl.

It's been my privilege to watch this portrait of an age grow piece by piece. Altogether, Tony gives us in these linked stories a rare glimpse of one boy's survival in a world gone mad with suffering. He has assembled a cast of characters worthy of Dickens—so various, so uniquely themselves—all the more astonishing because they are taken from life. It is a profound challenge, of course, to our humanity to see if we can hear these throwaway children on *their* terms, piecing together a life out of rubble.

As for AIDS, it is almost inconceivable that this plucky child with so much street smarts should have to bear this new scourge as well. But then, this monumental waste respects no limits, especially the notion that someone has had enough. Infuriatingly, Tony has been ineligible for lifesaving drugs because he doesn't fit the weight profile or the age profile. The system has discarded him.

And yet, for all he's been through, Tony Johnson writes without self-pity, so full of a life-giving enthusiasm that he can't help but share it. And he himself shares with the girl from Amsterdam a deep certainty about the essential goodness of people. He managed to make a new family for himself, and to draw together a band of fighters whose lives would be changed forever by their encounter with his extraordinary grace.

Go ahead, read him. He's not depressing at all. The failure to love isn't his, nor the failure of nerve that lets this tragedy go on and on. You will see how the heart makes room to live, even in the pitch of darkness. It is for us to see if we can turn his legacy into action, to make the fire of his words lighten the darkness.

—*Paul Monette*

# Introduction

It never occurred to me when I said, "Yes, I'd
love to," to Karen, the director of the children's
program at Northern Lights Alternatives, that
two days after my forty-ninth birthday I would
become a daddy. It was early October when
Karen called and asked whether I would be interested in talking with a thirteen-year-old boy recently diagnosed with AIDS. I asked why she had
chosen me, and she said she had talked with
several people about this kid and my name kept
coming up. She gave me a phone number, and
something remarkable, wonderful, and fun happened to my life: I met Tony Johnson.

My name is Jack Godby. I am currently an
HIV counselor. I am also a leader of the AIDS
Mastery workshops. I am into my seventh year
of being HIV-positive. At various times in my life
I have been an actor, a restaurant owner, a truck
driver, a druggie, even a baton-twirling champion. I'm gay, and since 1985, when my best
friend Gary Van Kirk was diagnosed with ARC,
I've had to face the challenge and horror of

AIDS. Before that, I was able to hold the nightmare happening around me at arm's length. And
then, more quickly than I realized, I could no
longer hide my head in fear.

I spoke with Tony after being interviewed, so
to speak, by his mother. She told me briefly
about the situation—how what she wanted for
Tony was someone outside the family whom he
could talk to without having to protect or take
care of. She told me about her family and how
Tony became a part of it. She asked if I would
like to say hello to him. I liked her voice—her
honesty—and trusted her concern and dedica-
tion to her son.

I almost held my breath as I introduced myself
to Tony that first time—nearly losing it when he
said, "I don't know you, and I'm not sure I want
to talk to you." Fair enough. Why *was* I talking
to him? He certainly was honest and straightfor-
ward. I liked that. I liked his clear voice and
soon realized that this was not a poor, helpless,
afflicted child to be coddled, but a very bright
young man with spunk, ideas, and most certainly
a voice of his own that needed to be heard. I
left it open for him to call me.

He did—ten minutes later. He wanted to know
what the deal was, whether he was becoming too
much for his family. Were they afraid they
couldn't cope with this new development in his
life? I assured him that was not the case, that
just what I'd told him in our first conversation
was true and that I didn't believe there were any

hidden motives. We talked about why it might be a good idea to have somebody he could just bitch to, if he wanted to. I began to wonder if I was up to him intellectually. He was quick to question anything I failed to make clear, and he didn't accept surface or clichéd answers, either. This was not going to be a "how ya doing, what's up, talk to you later" kind of relationship.

I would love to be able to recount our conversations with each other, because it may be difficult for you to imagine just how we progressed from telephone voices to a true sense of kinship. How can I explain Tony and myself, and what we have meant to each other, to people who don't know us? There are milestones like the first time we exchanged very heated obscenities at each other in an attempt to resolve the crisis arising from a sick social worker's misguided attempts to lay blame on Tony for his condition. Then there was the first time it was a "for nothing" call, just to say hi and ask how the day had gone. I won't forget the first time we said "I love you" to each other.

Joy seems to be a strange word to use when thinking or talking about Tony, but it is usually always what I feel. Tony has awakened my sense of play. My answering machine, with Tony's voice, states that Jack is "out playing." There's worry too, of the kind that I'm sure only one's child can bring. We learned to play together— sometimes for the fun of it, sometimes to make the pain and pressure of physical problems endurable. One night very late, we were dueling DJs, playing songs of the sixties and giggling because he knew the words. I never feel better than when I wander down a supermarket aisle, buying chips, popcorn, pretzels, corn twisters, two boxes of Entenmann's chocolate-chip cookies, seven Hershey bars, fun-size Three Musketeers, at least two pounds of M&M's, and assorted surprises like strawberries, pushcart pretzels that reek of charcoal, and requests for *Playboy* magazines and a beer. (He got root beer.) This is what Tony's weekly stash usually consists of, and even the strange looks of the checkout clerks couldn't dim my pleasure and excitement in getting these treats for him.

One night, as I held my breath while Frank, Tony's "body mechanic"—and subsequently my very good friend—cauterized a bleeder in his lung, Tony recited all of *Jonathan Livingston Seagull*. Thanks to "Northern Exposure," we have made numerous trips to Alaska, to go moose-watching and breathe the cold crisp air, or jump in an icy lake to help bring down a spiking fever. Every night ends with Tony laying his head on my shoulder, saying, "I love you like the good old days," and allowing me to sing him to sleep.

Tony's "Pop," his adoptive father, though he's been overseas for almost all the time I've known Tony, is always very present with us. As I groped along with early Daddyhood, my heart would relax when Tone would say, "Pop always says that," or "That's just what Pop would say." So it came as a complete surprise on November 9, 1991, when Tony decided that I needed another name besides Shithead. He asked how I liked "Big Daddy," and I said that would be okay and that I would call him the Applesauce Kid. (When he needs them, Tony takes painkillers in applesauce.) He went on to explain that this sort of made him my son. This was serious business—we both knew it—and I asked what Pop might think. He told me how Pop had two mothers—his mother and his grandmother—and that it had worked out just fine. Tony did in fact talk to his Pop about this, and happily reported that Pop had assured him it was wonderful and that his heart was big enough for both of us to share.

I've learned that having a son who is thirteen—going on fifty—is not to be taken lightly. It is an exercise in give-and-take, and we long ago dispensed with being polite to each other. We aren't afraid to talk about anything at any time. We have discussed religion, social injustice, the logistics of sex, the delights of Entenmann's chocolate-chip cookies, and death.

Death is not the same for me as it may be for other daddies. I don't have the luxury of putting off such a very painful topic. The specter of death has been with us from the beginning. Talking about it honestly with my brand-new son caused me to reexamine life. Tony has life. He is filled with the desire for all it has to offer.

He's told me often that these last few years with his new family have been the very best—Paradise, to be exact—and that he wouldn't trade them for anything. We keep looking at *right now*—at life. His gift to me is our constant striving to make our time together whole and complete, whether we are watching the Olympics or arguing over his not wanting dinner. There is no agenda, no format to follow. We just contend with what comes up—whatever it might be at that particular moment.

✓ Like it or not, life of course does include death. I freely admit to Tony that I don't know what happens when we die—and I just as freely admit, sometimes through tears, that I love him and will miss him so much. These admissions have occasionally caused Tony to want to pull away so that I would not have to endure this coming event. I reminded him—and maybe myself—what life would be like if we were so afraid of hurting that we chose not to risk loving. We chose to keep on risking—to keep on loving and sharing life on its own terms.

One night last January, Tony's lungs were filling up, and he had just undergone surgery that afternoon to relieve them. It was very painful and took a lot out of him. He went through it like the brave young man that he is. Later, however, a sneeze opened the incision. Frank told Tony's mom and me that he didn't think he could repair it and he didn't know whether Tony could endure the pain of another procedure. He said with a tear in his voice that he thought we should start a morphine drip. This was the moment we had known might come someday, and had dreaded. We knew we had to talk to Tony about what was happening to him—there are no secrets—and start the process of saying goodbye. When I got back on the phone with him, he asked me if he was going to die. I said, "I don't know, son." He, of course, picked up the tone of my voice and said, "We're in trouble, right?" Thank God his mom picked up the extension at that moment. We explained the situation quietly and mentioned the morphine drip. Tony asked what it was, and she said, "Something to help you sleep." Tony thought sleep was a good idea, and said so. She explained delicately that it would be deeper than that. There was a silence, followed by, "Oh, I get it—ASPCA." He said this in his brightest, clearest voice. There was another silence followed by his mom's and my nervous laughter. Tony said he wanted to know if anything could be done. Frank told him what he had told us, and that he just didn't know what the outcome would be. "No way!" Tony said. "Go for it, Frank." And we did.

Through our months together, Tony has told me a great deal about his life with "them"—we don't honor them with any other titles—those people who abused him so savagely and for so long. Many times it has been much easier for Tony to deal with his physical pain than to confront the emotional pain of the past. We handle these memories as they come up. We talk about them and work together to release their impact on the present. The fear is almost overpowering, and it takes trust and love for Tony to relive and conquer these brutal images. More than anything else, I wanted Tony to know he could trust me. I wanted a part in undoing the past lies, tricks, and pain. If it meant risking his anger or confronting his fear, so be it.

I believe that Tony is able to continue to let go of this past because of his innate innocence, a spirit that remained whole and pure, knowing that there was something better—something worth living for. As we have shared, laughed, and cried together, we have given each other much to live for.

I sometimes feel like a blind man in a minefield. If I don't actually step on a mine, my cane sets it off—that helpless feeling when a statement gets an unexpected reaction and I am already into full swing about how I'm going to save this one. How am I going to make him feel better? How am I going to help him understand? I can only keep telling my truths. I can only keep holding my son when he needs me. I can only be there when the past tries to eat away at our present. Tony and I are not martyrs or heroes. We are the Applesauce Kid and his Big Daddy, only doing our very best day by day—sometimes minute by minute—but only our very best.

I invite you in these pages to get to know my

son and to share his appetite for life. I know he will touch your heart. He will make you smile as you see his hope and gratitude and the power and promise that love brings.

—*Jack L. Godby*

# Asking for Wings

For most of my childhood I had the details of my goals well categorized in my mind, and I adhered to these stirring aspirations of tomorrow like a staunch follower of a sacred religion. When today is nothing outstanding to speak of, the future holds the most appeal, the most hope. It was all I had. Whether it was cocky self-possession or youthful delusion, I was positive that major-league baseball (preferably the New York Yankees) would inherit the best shortstop and power hitter in history. When that happened it would serve as a payback for all the unpleasantness I had to endure, all the atrocities I had to live. I was more than confident about this because I'd heard that things go in cycles. It stood to reason, then, that this was just the way things had to happen. Everything to follow *had* to be good. Thinking about that at my lowest moments made me feel better. Every struggle was worthwhile, every hardship felt like another step toward doing something I truly wanted to do. During my darkest moments, when it sometimes became necessary to remind myself that good things were on their way, I'd daydream about how fantastic it would be to make a six-figure salary doing something I enjoyed more than breathing.

I never felt so much alive as when I was on a makeshift baseball diamond. I was good. I knew it. When I stepped up to the plate, took my practice swings, and heard the scattered cheering and chanting of my name, an invigorating reassurance washed over those parts of me that were confused and hurt. As it was so aptly put by Sadaharu Oh, the legendary player for the Tokyo Giants, no one can stop a home run, and no one can understand what it really is. Therefore, he concluded, while you are on that diamond, it belongs to you only, and you are free from complication and demands. When I played baseball I felt that way; it made me feel that "someday" was more than a remote possibility. It was a promise. As the bat made contact and I'd watch the ball soar like a bullet over the fence, I advanced around the bases and felt every breath I took as the wind patted me firmly on the back.

My name is Tony. I'm fourteen—born in Manhattan in 1977, sneaking my way in with *Saturday Night Fever* and Debby Boone's endless "You Light Up My Life." That was the year that people were into genealogy—searching for their roots, thanks to the Alex Haley miniseries. It was apparent just what an impression it had made when, five years later, kindergarten registers bore names like Kizzy, LeVar, and Kunta Kinte. I was fortunate enough to see "Roots" recently, finishing up the last episode on the very day that Alex Haley died. I was deeply impressed at the legacy that he left while encouraging others to build their own legacies. That's a great deal of what my generation is about: finding the real person, the real heritage, the real life.

It took some time before I grasped who the real me was, and there are times still when I have trouble talking about myself. Sometimes I feel I am speaking of a stranger I have met casually. I've struggled and cried and thought seriously about killing myself. I've decided now to disclose the private corners of my thoughts, because people truly don't understand that being a kid and growing up is no easy task. I would love to stand face-to-face with the people who declare that childhood and adolescence are always the best times of a person's life. I'd be torn between wanting to make those people understand, and kicking them in the shins for being the biggest idiots in the world. In the following pages I'll introduce you to myself and other people my age who have grappled with today's rough, complex, and sometimes very nasty world. I was in a progressive education program in which the kids were all considered high caliber and gifted. But we were all torn by some shortcoming or disappointment in ourselves, in our homes, or in the world. While still very young, we fought battles over identity, sexuality, and survival. We wrestled with burnout, family problems, and the indecision of whether to live as a child or an adult.

In 1977 and later on, the baby boomers were winding down from making statements in the name of civil rights, women's lib, world peace, and ecology. It was a time when the world was moving haltingly, uncertain of its direction. For that reason, many of my contemporaries and I are the products of a generation that shrugs its shoulders a lot. We designate songs like "Don't Worry, Be Happy" as our anthems. It's not that we don't care, as the song lightheartedly suggests, it's just that we wear our hearts on our sleeves and we eat our hearts out. We smile when we do it, too. We've seldom been spared the atrocities of the times, and perhaps have become immune and more resigned to circumstances. We are not as quick or headstrong as the generation before us in believing that we can make a difference. We know too much. Unlike previous generations, in which things were not said "in front of the children," we've heard it all already. We know about cancer, nuclear war, the ozone layer, and AIDS. Fourth-grade classes are going to be taught about condom use. How many people of previous generations can say that they even knew what a condom was before they were sixteen? We don't have much time for innocence; innocence is for monks. There are too many issues that have direct effects on our lives and livelihoods. We have no choice but to take things in our stride. On occasion that attitude has taken good care of me. In some instances it has saved my life.

It's lucky for me that I grew up with the proper coping and survival skills. Otherwise I couldn't have made it in this very volatile, unpredictable world. Baby talk and nursery rhymes never had a place in my early life. Being born to people I feared more than anything in the world was my first clue about how difficult life actually was. To say that my life with them was ferocious would be to downplay that dreadful existence.

I have no desire to go into vivid details, because that life is behind me. Many parts of it can terrify me with the reality of their memory, but that time remains as real to me as anything else. I can attest that child abuse is alive and well and living all over this world—and is as close as New York City. Many people don't want to hear about it because it is too gruesome to imagine, and that attitude is sometimes just as bad as physically joining in the brutality. Turning a deaf ear has caused more casualties among the ranks of those defenseless and under eighteen than any war. If you think I'm exaggerating, check the statistics from hospital reports of those child-abuse cases that have been reported—and those classified as suspicious. That is to say nothing of those we don't know about. Abuse sends more kids to the emergency room than illness—and this information comes straight from the experts' mouths.

Many are the parents like mine, who see their

children as possessions and operate under the
guise of rightful ownership. They believe they
can do what they want with their children—and
they do. While there are those who strive to do
the best they can to see that their children have
the best upbringing possible, there are others
who don't give such things a thought; it's not a
priority and doesn't fit in with what their lives
are about.

The scariest part is that there is no way to
identify them. My parents weren't peculiar looking, and they weren't on welfare or uneducated.
My father held a job as a civil servant; my
mother could have been your next-door neighbor. Anyone who saw them would have smiled
approvingly because they *looked* so good. It's always been the norm to say that only minority
families are capable of these things. Would people be surprised.

That didn't change what was where I was concerned. Still waters run deep—and very dirty. My
parents were evil bullies who flourished with the
administration of pain and fear. They actually
derived pleasure from my needs and their unwill-
ingness to attend to them. I had no bed to sleep
in, and no warm coat in winter. I pretended for
years that I was eccentric and hated bulk on my
body, and that was why I layered myself with
sweatshirts. They usually belonged to my friend
David, who was two sizes bigger than I was. The
best meals I had were the ones at school that
other kids complained about constantly. If you

think such a situation is unbelievable, think again. When a kid is living with parents whose mindset is evil, anything is possible. If you can believe that a child can starve in a Third World country, and your heartstrings are being tugged enough to open your wallet, look as nearby as your next-door neighbor, whose kid is someone you wave to every day. Maybe he delivers your newspaper or offers to take your letters to the post office. Perhaps he is the kid who is always commended in the newspaper for academic or athletic skills. Maybe she made the cheerleading squad for the second year in a row. You don't have to live in a mud hut somewhere far away to go to bed hungry, cold, and afraid of what the next day might bring. Misery comes in all sizes and packages and does not discriminate geographically. Its unbiased distribution would truly astonish you.

My parents denied me Santa Claus, the tooth fairy, and stories about the Man in the Moon by forcing their own hateful world upon me on a daily basis. When other children in my first-grade class enthusiastically talked about what that wonderful man in the red suit would bring them for being good, I recalled silently how the year before I got a note stating that he would not be leaving anything for me because I had been a bad boy. I was relieved to find out shortly afterward that there was no such thing as Santa Claus anyway. He was just made up, like all of those other stupid stories we were told. It felt so much better not to have another enemy.

Since there was nothing within the confines of my life with my parents that ever resembled being easy, I expected nothing. While other kids were being tossed into the air, hugged and caressed, and lulled to sleep by their mothers, I was being flung into corners and slapped across rooms. The reasons never seemed to make sense. Perhaps I didn't answer quickly enough when someone called my name. Maybe I didn't perform a task correctly. As I look back on it, my parents' reasons for their behavior are as enraging as the actions themselves.

I guess I knew that everyone's life was not like mine when I began to notice my first-grade classmates being picked up after school while I ventured eight city blocks by myself every day. I was told that if anyone questioned this, I should say that my parents worked nights and could not come for me. As I watched those kids get hugged and kissed and told that they were missed, I thought about the night ahead of me and hoped that it would not be too difficult. I listened intently to the various ways that kids talked about their families, their lives, and their possessions, and I became quite good at doing the same thing. If a classmate got an Atari for Christmas, I said I had gotten one too. If their grandparents came to visit and brought presents, I nodded as if this were perfectly normal, and invented a gift of my own. I never initiated these conversations, so as not to leave myself open to have to prove my statements, but I was determined to keep my secret. No one could ever find out that I wasn't good enough to be like the rest.

By the time I was five, I realized that I was alone in this world and that it was up to me to see to my own survival. I made up my mind that I would do whatever it took. If it meant lying, I would lie. I have a vivid memory of being six years old and sitting on the stoop of the apartment building I lived in, making lists in huge block letters of wonderful things I wanted to have happen. At the top of the list I always wrote, "Get hugs and kisses like everyone else." After I finished a list, I would let it go and watch for a few minutes as it blew away through the air. I didn't realize there was no magic power out there that would read these wishes, and that they would be tossed into the trash along with the rest of the litter.

The four-room, tenth-floor apartment that we lived in on West 85th Street was not my home but theirs. I was entitled only to a space in the closet-sized back bedroom at the end of the hall. I slept on the floor there, sometimes on a flannel sheet, sometimes on the bare floorboards. I had a space in the corner where I kept the few articles of clothing I owned—usually the throwaways of other tenants. I had no toys or possessions, and my books were hidden in places at school because my father declared adamantly that only sissies read. I did homework spread out on that same floor, sometimes feeling stiff from the hardness of it. The king-sized bed in the huge bedroom at the front of the apartment belonged to them and was off limits to me at all times. So was the red velvet couch in the living room. There were no exceptions to this rule. Even if I was so tired that I couldn't see straight, I never entertained any thoughts of plopping down on the bed or the couch, because the consequences were not worth it. The contents of the refrigerator were theirs too, and I never had the luxury of just opening it up and raiding it as I had heard other kids talk about doing. Even the rhythm of the place was theirs—for their convenience. I was the one who was responsible for keeping everything clean, for getting the laundry done, and for doing whatever else they said I had to do. And there were consequences for rebelling against the rules.

My mother didn't care whether I slept or not. I had a toothbrush only because I got a free sample from a dental-care program at school. I was given permission to eat only on certain days of the week. My father said constantly that I had no right to things because I had not earned them. He also never made it clear how I was supposed to do that. He said that he was going to make a man out of me or kill me—and on too many occasions I couldn't even fake knowing what he was talking about. There was never any logical reason given for their actions except the harsh, vicious declarations that I was a "bad boy." Those words became as wearisome and emotionally tedious as the bruises that were regularly spread out on my body. Each time they said them, I struggled within myself to find the solution that would change their feelings toward me. I berated myself constantly because I could never manage to do anything that would buy me any kind of peace.

I was beaten often, because they said I deserved it. When I went without basic necessities, it was because I didn't deserve them. When sexual depravity occurred, they reasoned that such acts were my shortcomings—I made them do it because I wanted it. Did I? Maybe I did, I thought, because I didn't fight them hard enough. Could it be that I was missing something very simple, and that my own stupidity was causing this? I closed my mind when those things happened, sometimes praying to die. It all had to be true, I thought. After all, what but this kind of treatment can happen to anyone but a bad boy. With the sincere conviction of all that was inside me, I promised myself that I would do better—but it never worked, because there was never time for a reprieve.

They stopped at nothing to control my mind and body. They laughed at my pain; they took their best shots at my spirit and my soul. They made it clear that I was not safe, that I had better not become secure in anything. Not even as a slight consolation did they ever let me know that they loved me. Perhaps if they had, I might have been able to tolerate more.

I had a classmate named Carl who always talked about how his father beat him. But his father also bought him toys and took him to the park, and when he picked him up from school, he would hoist Carl onto his shoulder and laugh and play with him as they headed for home. Carl knew he had to stay clear when his father was drinking, and he was willing to take his chances because he was positive that his father loved him. I don't remember ever getting a hug or kiss from either of my parents. Their words were never kind. If I didn't feel well, I'd better not say so, because that would give them ammunition to attack me further. Their utter contempt and loathing of me reinforced my belief that I was nothing but a disturbing bone of contention. I didn't represent love or joy. They chose my life and my person as a reinforcement of who they were. I was someone they could rule, dominate, and overpower. I used to wonder in dread what would happen to me once they tired of me or were unable to bully me anymore. I doubted that I would be alive if that happened.

When I was about eight years old, a teacher brought *The Muppet Movie* to school. I sat mesmerized as I listened to the words of the song "Rainbow Connection." It gave me a sense of promise and told me in the simplest, most joyful way that we can seek out our own means to a beautiful life. If a frog could play a banjo and project such love, I, too, could have possibilities of the same things. I began to sing that song incessantly, to say the words over and over in my head every time things got so horrible that I would feel myself sinking.

One day, when my mother was in an uncharacteristically good mood, she heard me humming it as I sat by myself in the bedroom. She asked what it was, and I told her. I summoned the courage to ask her if, sometime when I was a good boy, she would get me a cassette of the soundtrack of the movie. There were cassette players at school and several of my friends had Walkmen. She said that as a matter of fact she wanted me to do something for her, and if I did, she would buy me the tape. I was thrilled. But I didn't realize until it was too late that what she wanted me to do was to allow her friend Jake to have his way with me sexually. That meant I would have to cooperate and not cry—no matter what Jake did, regardless of how much it hurt.

That type of request was not very unusual in their circle of acquaintances. They thrived on pain, particularly when it had to do with children, and even traded one another's children around to participate in bizarre rituals. To strip away at a child's soul gave them pleasure and a sense of power. It excited them, and consideration was never given to the inevitable toll it took.

Many parts of that experience with Jake draw a blank for me now, but I've always held on to bits and pieces of the pain and fear, and mostly my deep sense of worthlessness. How could I want anything so badly, I asked myself, that I would actually submit to such a thing? When I asked later on for the tape, my mother slapped me and denied that she had ever promised it. She said that I was to do what I was told, when I was told to do it, if I knew what was good for me. She ended the conversation by giving me a beating that left me bleeding and sore for several days. I swore that from then on I would never ask for anything again. I doubted that a bad boy like me could ever find a rainbow connection at all. There was too much rain to run interference.

It was during that time that I used to wonder if there was a God. If in fact there was, I wanted to be able to look into His eyes. All I had ever heard about Him were bits and pieces that kids talked about. You couldn't see or feel Him, but He was supposedly always there, watching us or punishing us or getting into our business. I couldn't talk about Him at home because He was considered an absolute nemesis. In school, people claimed that it was against my constitutional rights even to have a moment of silence with Him, and that only made me wonder what made Him so powerful that my constitutional rights had a role in it. My curiosity was fierce. Perhaps His eyes would give me a clue, at least, and tell me if He was real. They might reveal if the pain of the world was in them. I wanted to see, because if there was such a person, I'd know that He—the omnipotent being we learn to live in awe of—would reach out and touch the undried tears of an abused child and know his pain. He'd know the truth in the silence that the child was forced to maintain for the sake of his survival. That truth would speak for itself. He would see the shame in his eyes—a shame that he desperately fenced with more often than he cared to—a shame that opened the door to who the real boy was then and is now. If I saw God, I'd ask Him about freedom and tell Him that Thoreau was right when he said that birds don't sing in caves. People who are hurting don't sing either—because singing is a joy that comes from the freedom within the self that allows a person to fly. I'd ask Him for wings.

Hearing my story, you might think nothing good could come of a life like mine. I can imagine the questions about my sanity, my temperament, and my survival. You may want to know how such things can happen. My key to surviving has always been to keep a low profile and to maintain a sense that everything is all right. People don't want to make waves, and unfortunately many never try to crack the surface if it is appealing to the eye. Such was the case in my life. I did my homework, was respectful, and managed to be outwardly presentable—even if my insides were caving in.

I've seen other kids my age become hostile over experiences they've been forced to endure. I didn't come away from my experience unscathed. I'm not demure or mild-mannered when I'm feeling threatened; my temper can be explosive, and I'm stubborn and headstrong. Sometimes I can be rancorous enough to cut my nose off to spite my face, and much too often pride can be my first deadly sin. I have an ongoing battle with it.

I've never felt that the world did me wrong; I've always figured that it was just pretty messed up. I took good things from wherever I could get them, and sought my own comfort where I could find it. I made the decision that I would not be mean or hate. School served as my shelter from many storms.

Good fortune placed the best teachers in my midst. When most children cried in the first grade because they didn't want to leave their mothers, I sat at my desk eagerly and smiled back at the chubby, middle-aged woman with red hair, bright blue eyes, and the thickest Irish brogue I ever heard. She called us ladies and gentlemen and treated us with the utmost respect. She read us stories every day, and sometimes she surprised us with her homemade chocolate-chip cookies. She never raised her voice—with a roomful of forty first-graders it isn't easy—and she made the hours we spent in her class seem like a party that I never wanted to leave. Her kindness and patience taught me that it was so much better to be kind and patient. I realized that as long as I behaved myself and made an effort to do my schoolwork, that I could relax and things would run smoothly.

Teachers opened the doors to worlds for me that the rest of my life slammed shut. They saved me from the street. Because of them, I began to understand the concept of education and made the choice to persevere. They awakened me to the possibility of myself—my own potential—that would lead me toward a life I could build for myself. They managed to show me, each in his or her own unique way, that my own creativity had a great deal to do with the way I handled pain and vulnerability. They provided hope in the knowledge that I would have the luxury of claiming my mind as my own. They introduced me to "someday"—my only concrete weapon against the nightmare. I was receptive to it all because I wanted it so desperately.

I wish I could say thank you to everyone who has helped me on the road to becoming myself. Since that is nearly impossible, I'll do what I can to continue the cycle of their good teaching. I begin with Mister Rogers. Yes, I know all the jokes connected with him—the sneakers and the sweater and the beautiful day in the neighborhood—and I even laugh a little when Eddie Murphy makes fun of him as Mister Robinson. Nothing, however, could take away from the fact that he was the first friend I ever had. His show would come on at seven-thirty in the morning, long before my parents showed signs of getting up. As I sat on the floor glued to the TV for thirty minutes, nothing else mattered. I *believed* that he was my neighbor, was *positive* that he was talking to *me* when he smiled and explained things so gently. More than once I imagined him holding me close to him. During those times when I was most afraid, it was his silly songs that were my salvation. Their words relayed what I wanted—and so desperately *needed*—to hear. He emphasized the value of people. His words convinced me that *I* was important and that he liked me for myself. Being someone's neighbor sustained me and gave me the incentive to believe in myself, in kindness, and in sharing. When I was in Mister Rogers' Neighborhood there was time for awe and wonder. There was room for love. I listened intently to every word, every story, I sang along with every song—and when the show was over, I waved good-bye and believed with all my heart that he would be back, because I figured that when someone loved you, he'd always come back.

While I choose not to make light of the horror or hard times I lived through—they are things that should never go overlooked for any child—I hope this book can serve as a celebration of life, a picture of me, just an ordinary kid with hopes and dreams, fantasies and wishes, looking to make a mark.

For the last few years I have had a loving family. I got lucky one evening when I called a hot line and told a man on the other end that I had no option except to kill myself. It had been a horrible day that began with a beating that was halted with the promise of another later in the evening. All day I could barely get from one class to another because I felt so terrible. My head hurt, I had chills, and I wanted to go to sleep and not wake up. I wondered where it would be safe even to do that. I half-listened to my teachers as I contemplated different methods of suicide. I thought about walking in front of a bus that was going full speed, stepping off into the subway tracks as the train was coming, or cutting my wrists. I wanted it to be over and I no longer cared about blowing my cover with teachers, friends, or anyone else.

I had managed until now to keep questions and concern at bay. No one at school suspected that anything was wrong at home because I excelled in my work and kept a low profile. I never rebelled against taking physical education, and I covered up bruises with long sweats. I was amiable, although I never allowed anyone to get close enough to exceed courtesy. Luckily—or unluckily—school officials were too busy nosing into the business of dysfunctional minority families. On this particular day, the jig was up. The secret could stay inside me no longer, and I was going to end it by ending my life. I decided I wanted to tell someone, even a stranger, that there was once a kid named Tony who lived in this world. A nationwide hot line seemed a good enough way to do it.

The pronounced Southern drawl on the other

end of the phone belonged to someone I would soon begin to call Pop. It became one of the most familiar and cherished voices in my life. It promised to bring comfort and protection. It made me smile. As I stood at a telephone booth at 85th Street and Amsterdam Avenue, oblivious to the weird going-ons and the noise of the people, I poured my troubles out to this man and cried in a way I had never done before. He listened, stopping me occasionally to ask something. His voice was gentle and low, and I could almost feel him reaching through the wires to hold me. He made it clear that he was determined to help me through this seemingly hopeless situation. The last thing that he said to me before we hung up was, "I promise we'll do something." Even as all of my bitter skepticism warned me against it, I believed him.

I should have known who this man was—someone who refused ever to give in to adversity. When he said that we would "kick ass and take names," he meant it. It's not hard to understand why he did so well as a career military man. He is disciplined and exact, extremely methodical and no-nonsense. He fears nothing and no one. However, he balances this with kindness and gentleness—a tenderness that lets you know his heart is far from unbreakable. It's in the look in his eyes, the firmness of his grip when he holds me close to him, the soft whisper when his face touches mine and he asks, "What's the matter, son?" Those traits have saved my life on many occasions.

On that very evening when I hooked up with Pop, I found Mom, too, a lady with the most beautiful smiling blue eyes I had ever seen. If you ever want a scale model of a mom, take your characteristics from her. Her soft-spokenness soothes me. Her quiet inner strength and capacity for quick thinking and common sense is the glue that keeps our family firmly together. Mom's was a referral number in Pop's computer. I promised I'd call her and then call him back once she directed me someplace.

I liked her immediately when we began to talk, because she was neither scary nor condescending. She asked me to meet her for coffee, just so that we'd be able to talk face-to-face. She promised there would be no tricks, that I could leave at any point. She reasoned that if I was going to kill myself anyway, what difference would a half hour make? I agreed to meet her at 54th and Broadway.

Her smile was the first thing that caught me. I'd somehow imagined that it would be wonderful, because I could hear it in her voice. It was genuine, and if in fact the eyes are the windows of the soul, I knew that her soul had to be pure.

It didn't take long to acknowledge that our conversation was making sense. Her opinion was that I wouldn't be able to resolve anything about the disarray of my life until I felt a little better physically. I admitted to her that I had been beaten pretty badly early that morning. I had never said those words to anyone, but she didn't seem to hate me at all for it. On the contrary, she said that she was afraid for me! I tried to tell her I didn't think about being afraid. I found myself reverting to my habit of pretending that I was all right. If that was true, she asked, why did I feel so trapped, and why was I trying so hard to convince her that I wasn't afraid? My silence told her that I *was* afraid and that I just didn't want to allow myself to know the fear. She said I deserved better and that it upset her to know that if I chose not to take her help, my father might kill me. She promised to work in my corner every step of the way, and that she'd do whatever was humanly possible to see that no one ever hurt me again. For the second time in a day, I believed someone. No one had ever committed any promises to me as the two of them did that night.

When we went outside to get into her car, she unlocked the door but allowed me to open it and get inside myself. When she got in on the driver's side, she very casually twisted all of the heat vents in my direction, then turned the key in the ignition. I looked closely at the photo button hanging from a ribbon on the rearview mirror: two smiling little girls in ponytails, with their arms around each other. She smiled proudly and told me that they were her daughters, who were nine and seven. My gaze fixed on those smiles; they were as happy as hers.

I dozed as we drove to the hospital, surprised that I could actually get comfortable. She reached into the backseat when we stopped at a stoplight, and pulled a bulky blue afghan to the front. As she spread it out over me, someone honked a horn because she was stopping traffic. The light had changed while she positioned it just so. She saw that the horn made me nervous, and said that they could wait a minute—my first indication that she was not one to bend to pressure. I thanked her and she smiled. Then she turned to an oldies station on the radio, and I could hear her singing softly as I drifted in and out of sleep. For the first time in my life I was relaxed and not terrified that something horrible would happen to me. I don't know whether it was because I had made the decision to die, or whether she represented my one last possibility to live. I tend to believe it was the latter.

When we arrived at the hospital, she immediately got me through the crowded emergency room and I was taken to a draped section of the treatment room. She sounded official and knowledgeable, and insisted that the doctors and nurses explain what they were doing. The poking and prodding and various tests seemed endless, as did the questions and concerned looks from several different doctors. She talked me into staying, saying that a good night's sleep would help me make better decisions, and promised to be back to see me first thing in the morning. Then she took Pop's phone number and assured me that she would call and tell him that I was there. That's how the nightmare slowly faded and my life began.

Mom and Pop got to know each other as they simultaneously took an interest in me. After she called him and told him where I was, he flew into New York three days later. I noticed that the two of them were always talking together and consulting with the different hospital staff members. They took turns staying with me, and when I fell asleep, they talked and shared meals together. I remember waking up once and giggling when I saw them seated across from each other, using my meal tray to lay out their cards as they battled out a gin rummy game.

He fell hard in love with her. Later he admitted that this was the closest he had ever come to falling in love at first sight. He said he didn't think there was anyone in this world that he could love as much. He hadn't thought that he would ever hook up with such a gentle woman.

Mom had a similar impression of him. They both had suffered through horrendous marriages and breakups, and each of them had two children—his grown, hers still in elementary school. Pop is ten years older than Mom. She is white, and a New York City girl. Raised in a loving yet modest home, the youngest of five children, she is also the only girl in the family, and often shakes her head in tolerant protest that her brothers still have not gotten it through their heads that she is no longer their baby sister. I love their relationship. She and her brothers hug and kiss hello and good-bye. They are actively involved in one another's lives, and it's obvious to onlookers that this is an exclusive group. Before them, I never saw brothers kiss one another in greeting in such an uninhibited manner.

Mom talks often about the security of the home she grew up in. Her family wasn't wealthy; they lived in a basement apartment in upper Manhattan. Most of their furniture was other tenants' throwaways. They didn't know the difference, but they did know that they loved one another. The greatest times I have ever had were when I have sat listening to Mom and her brothers reminisce about different things, from parties and weddings and funerals to everyday goings-on in their home. These memories, some significant, some simple, have made them wonderful adults, and they shine through in everything that Mom does.

Pop is black and was raised in Stamps, Arkansas, during the civil rights upheavals of the sixties. He's most comfortable in wide open spaces in the country. He's a big man—the product of heredity and a rigorous workout schedule. His smile is like that of a bashful six-year-old. His laugh is hearty, his speech scattered with charming colloquialisms: "We might could do that," or "I'm fixing to leave now." Though I tease him unmercifully about it, I love the way he talks. It's such an essential part of him. He was raised mostly by his paternal grandmother, a retired schoolteacher whom he calls Mama. She took him to church every Sunday, and she made him study. As a boy, he wanted to become an astronomer, but he chose instead a career in the military, because there he could get the education that otherwise he might not. His twenty-five years in the service took him all over the world, to places he speaks of with reverence and wonder. Ask him where home is, though, and he'll tell you that it's Stamps, where he can eat chitlins and cornbread and lie in a hammock. He loathes New York—the accent, the concept, and the life-style. He calls it a jungle. He loves Mom, though, and has said more than once that he'd pitch a tent in the middle of Times Square to be with her.

From the start they strove together to make a stable home life for me. Both were determined to keep their promise that I would never have to go back to the nightmare. Whenever I asked Pop what was going to happen to me, he would always respond by saying, "You just let us take care of that." They swore that even if they had to sneak me out of the country, I would never have to go back. Aggressively they challenged doctors, social workers, and courts. Neither of them could be intimidated easily, nor did they back down from the challenge of protecting me. I had already begun to call them Mom and Pop, and they treated me as if I were theirs forever.

There were times, however, when I wondered what I had gotten myself into. As I rested against the pillows and took in the peace and quiet, I still doubted sometimes that I was out of danger. It seemed as if the more comfortable I got, the edgier I became. One night Mom and Pop were whispering quietly about me when they thought that I was asleep. They were talking about our next bout in court. "He keeps asking me what's going to happen to him," Pop said, "and I don't know what to tell him."

Mom was as casual and matter-of-fact as always. "We've told him that we would take care of him, and we will."

Pop sighed. "I hope I don't have to break too many heads open, because I will."

While there was security in knowing that they would persist, unpleasant memories caused me to feel a helplessness and fright that I often struggled with. My father had always said I would never get away. If I ever tried, he swore he would hunt me down and kill me. He promised that it would be slow and painful. While my new parents were assuring me that nothing bad could happen to me, I was flooded with terrified visions of the old ones, who I knew delighted in their own ruthlessness. I had already made my mind up that if the courts decided I had to go back with them, this time I would indeed kill myself, and I would do it silently and quickly. Having been given a reprieve from that life, I knew I could never go back again. It was a happy day in my life when Mom and Pop walked into that hospital room and announced that they

were legally my parents. My last name was
Pop's—I was his son, he told me proudly as he
held me close to him. A lump still forms in my
throat when I remember that day.

There were still a few legal battles to come,
though. My parents would be made to pay for
their actions, and I would have to talk with a
judge and tell what my life had been like. Pop
and I talked for a long time the morning we first
went to court. I told him that I was afraid—that
it made my insides shake to have to see them
once more.

"You just hold on to me, son. No one's going
to get near you, I promise that."

I began to cry. "They scare me so bad, Pop, I
can't even stand up straight."

"That's because you never had me right there
with you to hold you up. I'm your father now,
and I take that honor very seriously."

It didn't take the haggling that I thought it
would in the courtroom. After a few minutes of
discussion between the two lawyers, the judge
asked to talk to me. We went into a room together, and he told me to sit down. He asked
the clerk to get us a snack, and we talked. He
asked me questions about my parents and the
things they had done to me. He wanted to know
if I thought I would be happy with Mom and
Pop, and I told him I had never been happier
than during this short time I had been with
them. He shook my hand and wished me luck.
I went back to sit next to Pop, and the judge

came out and spoke about the horrors they had forced me to endure and said they wouldn't get away with it if he had anything to say about it.

Ultimately, both were convicted of abuse and sent to prison and I would never have to see them again. All I had left to do was to insist that the nightmare disappear, and I had the rest of my life to do it.

Shortly after that, Pop proposed to Mom and she agreed to marry him. I can't say that their union has ever surprised me, because from the start it was obvious that the two of them clicked. Although they were from different cultures, different parts of the country, virtually different worlds, they had more in common than many couples who had been raised in the same neighborhood.

It was a mind-boggling relief to be secure in a new home. Not only did I have real parents, but a brother and sister from one side and two sisters from the other. My sisters, Robin and Gina, became my fast friends. Robin and I share a birthday and some of the same traits. Robin loves horror movies and things that will scare the hell out of her. Pop says that's good, that she's healthy and fearless. One of the best times we shared last summer was reading Stephen King's *Misery* while everyone else in the house was asleep. Since I had read it already, I picked out the most gruesome spots for her to read aloud. I won't mention here the names that she called me because of it. She tried to think of ways to get even with me for weeks. To this day she promises that she will.

Gina is the complete opposite of Robin and me. She's sensitive and a pacifist, always ready to negotiate compromises. If something is going to cause a problem or a fight, she doesn't want to hear about it because she'll already have decided that it's not worth it. That is, of course, as long as it doesn't have to do with an animal. We tease her by calling her Miss Wild Kingdom, because she's big on animal protection and rights. She once tried to talk Mom into adopting a pig to save it from the butcher. She wanted a baby bear that was rescued from the wilderness. She talks to her dog as if he were a baby, and she feeds stray cats that come into the backyard. She's self-possessed enough to tolerate our ragging, though, and that's why I like her so much.

When I first went to live with my new family, there were still many things wrong with me. According to one doctor's explanation, I was making up for lost time. Years of indiscriminately taking aspirin (I thought it was a cure for everything, and bought bottles of two hundred), not eating right, and general neglect had caught up with me. Many doctors asked me, baffled, "Didn't you realize that you just didn't feel good?" Of course I had realized it, but there wasn't a great deal I could actually do about it. Until this time I had never even been seen by a doctor. They discovered I had fifty-four badly healed bones. I had an advanced case of syphilis, a disease I had heard about only in passing; I had read somewhere that Al Capone died of it. The doctors said that I was lucky they had caught it, but that it had already begun to take its toll on major organs in my body—mainly my lungs. I wish I had a buck for every time I had pneumonia. The heaviness in my chest—and in Mom's and Pop's eyes—would always signal the onset. They would camp in my bedroom and take turns caring for me. I already knew to expect those large, invasive needles that the doctor used to get fluid out. Often Pop would rub me down with alcohol and ice to lower my constant fevers. Those were the times when they combined their effort, patience, and know-how to get me through. I found myself apologizing to them many times, though both of them told me there was no need, and I believed them. They were determined to make me healthy, no matter how long it took or how hard it was. Pop said we were "kicking ass and taking names"—on our way to getting on the "good foot."

Being with them was like living in Paradise. From the first day, Mom did everything she could to make me feel special. Some were little things, like making sure that my bed and pillows were fixed just so, that my shirts were soft and smelled fresh. She made delicious things to eat and was happiest when I ate like a pig. On nights when I couldn't sleep, Mom took out coloring books and crayons, turned on some soft music, and we colored together. I've always enjoyed coloring, and many times the sun would be coming up when we were just about finished with our books. She was always willing to talk, and she refused to insult me with sugar-coated lies. It was just logical to her that we would deal with the cards in our hands and that there was no room for secrets. They weren't necessary. That didn't mean, though, that I had to talk. I learned fast with her that there weren't many "have to"s. It made me trust her, even when things were at their worst. I wasn't so afraid anymore. I asked her several times if she thought I would die. She never said no, but she always assured me that, whatever happened, we would all deal with it together. Mom has a wonderful sense of quiet; often it isn't necessary for her to say anything at all, because her love shines through. During a snowstorm once, I was lying in bed moping because I couldn't get up. Mom came in from shopping and picked me up. "You've got to see this!" she said. I sat on her lap on the window seat and we watched the snow fall for several minutes. We said nothing, but didn't have to. She felt soft, and her familiar scent of violet cologne was so comforting. What words could have described that?

Pop was always there to remind me of all of the great things we had yet to do. He talked of trips, ball games, and our lives together. When I got cranky, he would launch into song, not stopping until I sang with him. One night I refused to join in. I looked at him with annoyance and asked him to cut it out. That's when he began to sing at the top of his lungs, "If you want to be happy for the rest of your life, never make a pretty woman your wife." We laughed at Mom's reaction, and got hysterical when the nurses asked him to shut up. My eyes fill with tears every time I hear "Gypsy Woman"; it is the song that got the most wear from us. He began to sing it one night as I lay against his chest, the pain in my head so severe that I couldn't stop shaking. He sang it in a mellow, blueslike fashion, obviously very taken with the lyrics. I sang back with him before long; this was to become our equalizer. Pop confided in me that the gypsy woman he sings about loving so much is Mom.

Once a doctor told Pop that I would not make it out of a coma—that it was God's will. Pop said loudly that God was going to have to go through him. Taking me in his arms, he began to sing the song over and over. Just as a nurse was telling Mom to get him away from me, that he was uselessly torturing himself, I began to sing with him. The doctors and nurses were surprised, but Pop wasn't.

"Nothing in this world matters but love," he says emphatically. He has a copy of *The Velveteen Rabbit* on hand with him everywhere he goes. It's a conviction that he lives by—a love that showed itself on those long nights when he would lie in bed beside me and read poetry. I learned that we loved the same poems: "Invictus," "If," and "Casey at the Bat." We have both read *Jonathan Livingston Seagull* over and over until we memorized it. Because of the unfortunate ending of "Casey at the Bat" ("There is no joy in Mudville, Mighty Casey has struck out"), Pop made up his own version on the spur of the moment, while I was going through an arduous lung-tapping—and renamed it "Tony-Bob at the Bat." While tears ran down my face from pain and fear, Pop squatted so as to be eye-level with me. Using the best sportscaster's voice he could muster, he began to improvise. In Pop's version, unlike the original Casey, I save the game with a grand slam home run.

Pop took to calling me Tony-Bob because he said that a nice, down-home Southern name would keep me honest. It's his special term of affection for me that seals an exclusive intimacy in our relationship. It was that same intimacy that got me on my feet again after I had a stroke that paralyzed my left side. The doctors couldn't really explain how it happened, except to surmise that years of aspirin abuse and extremely high fevers made it inevitable. Pop insisted, despite the adamant disagreement of specialists, that I *would* get up and walk. He bought me my first baseball glove and bat, and was determined that I would use them. He promised that as he exercised the limp muscles in my arm and leg twice a day. He began a regimen in which we would get up before anyone else was awake and work out. He'd place me on the weight bench in the basement, chant obscene military cadences, and make me chant back. We'd laugh so much that I never realized how hard we were working.

I learned a great deal about family during that time as everyone rallied together with the common goal of getting me back on my feet. Robin and Gina would help with arm and finger exercises. Mom gave me several massages a day, and we had great conversations as she did it. She talked about my sisters and the things they had done when they were little. Her brothers, my uncles Joe and Sam, would come over and play Nerf basketball with me. Uncle Bill sent me a pair of Pump sneakers to give me an incentive to get up. Uncle Mike brought me a peashooter.

The time came when Pop was positive I could walk. He knew that I was afraid—terrified, actually—that I would fall and embarrassed that I wouldn't be able to move. He insisted that I would walk—all of the training as a sergeant was present that day—that I had to. I clung stubbornly to the side of the bed, tears welling in my eyes.

"You're going to cut out that crying," he said firmly, "and you're going to get your ass up and strut your stuff. If you fall, you'll get up and try again!"

"I'm not," I countered as I looked up at Mom, hoping to evoke sympathy.

At that, Pop whisked me up in his arms. "Forget about your mama. Time to get on the good foot!" Gently he carried me out into the backyard and placed me on the ground. "Come on, Tony-

Bob. It's springtime! Are you about to let it pass you by?" He pointed to an old chestnut tree. "Go take a leak on that ugly tree. I'll take one with you."

I looked up at his face and he was smiling. He extended his hand and I clutched it tightly. I took one step, then another, then three more. He was nodding proudly, kindly encouraging me to go on. After a few moments he let go of my hand and I made it to the tree by myself. As I turned to look at him again, there was victory written all over his face. I knew I was on the road. Pop knew it, too. Life would be sweet from here on in.

Pop and I did pee on that tree, amid much head-shaking and groaning (and, I suspect, hidden amusement) from Mom. We shook hands and he hugged me. Then our eyes met and he said gravely, "Every victory for you means one more that they lose." Of course, he was referring to the demons of yesterday. I felt, as he did, that we were well on our way to kicking ass and taking names. I had no desire to look back.

There were holidays and birthday parties. I got to go to a dance, to a military banquet, on vacation. I rode a roller coaster and went to a Halloween party. I spent Christmas Eve helping Pop put toys together for the girls as we ate chocolate and listened to Christmas carols. I attended two different Christmas services.

I had been in a progressive school program for four years, and that paid off too. I got my high school diploma through tutors and had begun to look into options for college. A major university offered me a four-year scholarship, and I was pondering choices. Each day was an adventure, a declaration of freedom and strength. The rest of my life promised to iron out the details. Mom and Pop were willing to do whatever it took to assure that.

Then AIDS made its introduction.

For the preceding two years, each time I was tested, the results had come back negative. They say that happens sometimes. It must be someone's idea of a sick joke. I recalled once again the episode with Jake. It was no different from any others I had endured since I was very young. No different except for what happened a few weeks after the incident. I overheard laughter and his name mentioned. Someone was mockingly saying that the poor bastard had AIDS. I knew very little about AIDS, and certainly didn't grasp the humor. When I was diagnosed, however, I was convinced that it was all my fault because I hadn't done enough to stop it from happening. I'd bought myself a life sentence, looking for my rainbow connection.

I should have known that something horrible was imminent. I didn't feel right, particularly when I woke up two or three times a night to change my sweat-soaked T-shirts. I noticed, although I brushed if off and didn't tell anyone, that I got out of breath a great deal and that my energy level was low. What confirmed things was the onset of an opportunistic infection. It's amazing how quickly we learn the terminology. The first time I heard the initials PCP, I thought of angel dust and was already making a case for myself that I had never touched it. I soon learned that it was pneumocystis pneumonia.

√ Those people who believe that AIDS is a condemnation from God should be in a room with someone just hearing his or her diagnosis. In his book *Borrowed Time*, Paul Monette talks about how devastating it is: "Your eyes are too shut to cry." Think about how bad that can feel. It goes beyond tears, beyond hysterics. It's like a deafening silence that falls over a room and makes people look as if they have had the wind knocked out of them. I wish I had a freeze-frame shot of Pop's eyes the day he struggled to find the words to diminish the impact of the news he was about to deliver. Mom was the one who ended up saying the words, because he couldn't. Maybe a good look at both their faces would bring into focus the fact that AIDS is a killer—a virus that attacks a body bit by bit and tears apart a family in the process. I know that I am advocating now. I have had to endure the prejudices of a frightened and uninformed public. I had planned to spend the rest of my life thankful for being able to live my "someday." But now that it's here, I have no clue to its length.

I've gotten wishy-washy. I smile and become teary at poignant moments because it's always in the back of my mind that there might be very few more. I think of Mom and Pop lying on the couch next to each other, watching a video of Natalie Cole singing "Unforgettable." He bends over her and sings the song as he kisses her head. They are stealing a moment that is exclusively theirs until it is time to get on with this new nightmare. The military has recently called Pop into temporary duty, and it's hard to know when we'll see him next. I've come to know that the pain of separation is never so apparent as when you are reunited with the one you love the most. I realized that when Pop embraced Mom after a long separation. The tension in his knuckles as he held her, the relief on his face at seeing her—only true love can make that happen. I'm angry that I'll never experience it. It makes me so sad to know that when I say "I'll see you," I'm not sure I will.

I live on the moon now—and the way things look, unless someone very learned in research moves his ass to happen upon a cure, that's where I'm staying. I should explain. "Living on the moon" is a phrase that Paul Monette coined to emphasize how, because of the lack of love, understanding, and help, those of us with AIDS have been made to feel distant from and out of touch with those who don't have it. But they're a loyal bunch, those who live there with me. Their sentiments are true and heartfelt—never in need of publicity. They're not afraid to hold me or kiss me or help me weather some of the horrors that

AIDS brings. I still would do anything to get well.

A wonderful thing happened as a result of my newly discovered HIV-positive status. I got myself a dad. We met some months ago when Mom phoned a place called Northern Lights Alternatives to ask about a volunteer to help me through the transition period of finding out I had AIDS. She felt that I was holding too much inside, and hoped that an outsider could help me to say whatever I wanted to say when things got too difficult.

Our first conversation went something like this:

"Hi. My name is Jack and I wanted to call and say hi to you and also to tell you that I'm available if you ever need to talk."

If he had seen the filthy look that I gave him, he would have hung up the phone. I never needed anyone to seek out friends for me, and I had already begun to rehearse in my mind what I would say to Mom that would amount to telling her to stay out of my life. "I don't know you," I said rudely, "and I don't think I want to talk to you."

He wasn't intimidated by me at all though, and continued to talk, telling me about himself. He was an ex-actor who had a great laugh and a voice like that of a radio announcer. Still, I refused to like him—even when he gave me his home and work numbers and told me to call whenever I wanted to. We hung up—he said something about calling again later that week—and I called him ten minutes later to ask him what the deal was. I didn't want anyone to like me. I certainly didn't want to make any new friends. All I wanted was a quick and easy way to put myself out of my own misery. I figured that the best thing I could do for myself would be to cut my losses and fade out without any bangs. But I had to admit that my life had turned out to be much better than I'd ever imagined it could be. A part of me—the largest and most alive part of me—wanted to go on. I suppose that's why I listened when he talked about how important it was to live for right now. "Right now we're talking, we were just laughing—passing time pretty good. We don't need to go any further than we have to." Dammit! He made sense! And so he opened the door to one of the most cherished relationships of my life.

Over the next few weeks, the two of us got to know each other a little better. Jack's disposition is similar to mine; he is intolerant of phonies. He genuinely likes people, though, and I like that about him. A great many passions run through him, yet to use his favorite phrase, he is no "drama queen." Whenever he becomes moved, it is not theatrical but sincere. He *celebrates* emotions, allowing them to do whatever they need to do. I learned from him to do the same thing.

Once, a social worker took it upon herself to "save" me. It's incredible how many value judgments exist around AIDS. She said that AIDS was a punishment for wrongdoing, and she wanted me to repent for my sins. Jack was outraged. He began to take active care of me, to look out for my needs and feelings, and to cushion each blow as it fell—and there were many. The ugly and frightening reality of AIDS had begun to present itself, and the issues grew more complicated. There were medical procedures and symptoms, sometimes uncontrollable pain. Then there was rejection—people's obvious aversion to me. One night, when I became overwhelmed by all that had been happening at such a rapid pace, he said, "You know, you don't have to do this by yourself, baby." Such was his gentleness that I chose to take him up on his offer to be there with me. I was glad he had signed on for the ride. When he went on a business trip for four days, it occurred to me that I truly missed him. It hit me how very much I loved him. There was a fledgling trust between us. I knew this journey—whatever it might bring—would be shared. There is nothing that can scare him away, and he continually demonstrates that.

On November 9, 1991, I decided that he needed a new name—one that was his alone. I told him I would call him "Big Daddy." Pop called his grandfather that name because he was the patriarch that everyone loved. Before that day, it had never felt safe for me to call anyone that name. God knows I loved Pop, but I couldn't bring myself to call him Dad. The name was just too painful. It wasn't that my new dad could help me overcome anything that Pop couldn't, but it had begun to occur to me that I was safe and that there were no ghosts that could interfere. I told Pop about what I had renamed Jack, a little concerned that he might feel rejected.

"I'll always be your Pop," he said. "You can't ever get too much love." He went on to tell me that he had two mothers: his biological mother and his paternal grandmother. He called them both Mama, loved them both dearly. He told me to hold on tight to my Daddy and to be happy that I have him.

Ours is not a relationship of hearts and flowers. Sometimes it's blood and guts and war. We've had screaming and shouting matches. We've also cried and held each other. Every week he sends me a stash of Hershey bars, M&M's, all kinds of chips, and lots of cookies. He wants me to be well stocked for our TV nights. While we watch "Murphy Brown," "Designing Women," and "Northern Exposure," I devour my assortment of junk, and Dad keeps a careful watch on his cholesterol level and enjoys my snacks vicariously. His doctor declares that in this age of AIDS he will not allow him to die of a heart attack.

There's more to Dad than sitcoms and junk food. In this short time I can close my eyes and think of many things about him that have changed my life forever. He's told me that doormats are suited only for muddy shoes, and thanks to him,

I never think in terms of forever. He has shown me that if I take care of the present, I take care of forever at the same time, and that I can use the ugliness of the past to help me become a better person.

When I was so frightened as a little kid and I never knew what would become of me, I used to fantasize about a hero who would come along to rescue me from the monsters. He would look like an ordinary person, wear ordinary clothes, and live in a house, not a faraway planet or a cave. Ideally, he would love me. Well, I have found him. In the time we have been together, my Dad has made dreams come true. He knew I had always wanted a kitten, so he combed New York City and found me one. He goes into toy stores and buys things—practical and impractical—and makes me feel like I have won some kind of grand prize. He insists that we don't postpone joy, and sees to it every day that we both remember that. There's no magic formula, he just loves me, and that's all I have ever wanted.

Through our games, our contending with things that are unpleasant, and our vigorous living of every day, we choose to push away from whatever tampers with our capacity for love. We're doing life—whether we're talking seriously or watching "The Simpsons."

My Dad was one of the people who encouraged me to write this book. It's the story of how one kid lived his life, before AIDS and after. I want to tell you stories about my friends at school, about other people I knew, and about how tough it was for all of us to grow up—but how good things could be too. I'll tell you about Mom and Pop and Dad, and what living with AIDS has been like. I don't want to tell you stories that will make you sad, because I have had very happy moments. I'm very grateful for the life I have made for myself and that others have helped me to make. While some things have been difficult, nothing can diminish the fact that I am here and glad to be. Come and celebrate with me.

# David, Times Square, and Forever

If we're lucky, we all find one friend who loves us purely for who we are. That friend won't always like everything we do, and may disagree with many of our opinions and tastes. Such was my best friend, David. He often said I drove him crazy, that he didn't know why he hung out with me so much. He had this way of shrugging his shoulders and rolling his eyes that meant he had had as much as he could take from anyone. Yet that never disturbed me. I'd smile and tell him to shut up—self-assured that I could be whoever I was. I could be silly, or distant, angry, and moody. So could he. We were positive of each other's loyalty. The obstacles we faced were often harrowing, but we took comfort in each other's presence. Somehow, knowing that David was around, I could convince myself that there was reason to go on. We depended on each other for security and stability. It wasn't that we could make things wonderful or all better, either. It's just that we could manage during very trying circumstances. I knew that David was the one person who would walk through the fire with me if someone had to.

I have a photograph of the two of us taken at a school function. His arm is around my shoulder and we're smiling, obviously comfortable with each other. We look like a brotherhood ad—David, dark and bearing some of his father's black features, I resembling the standard all-American boy, with fair skin, blondish hair, and blue eyes. David was closer to me than any brother could be. We fought like brothers, too. I can recount the times when he told me that I made him sick and that I was a naive idiot who would understand "real life" someday.

We met in the fourth grade when some classmates instigated a fight between us. I don't remember what the fight was supposed to be about, I just knew that when the dismissal bell rang, each of us was on a mission to send the other to his grave. Two teachers were in the schoolyard conversing as we glared at each other. The usual threats ensued, and the teachers, oblivious to us, showed no signs of winding down their bull session. After about forty minutes, the other kids, who had hung around like a bunch of fight enthusiasts at Madison Square Garden, lost interest and went home.

While the teachers continued to talk, David and I looked at each other and grinned sheepishly as we realized that we had been designated the fools of the afternoon, who had bought into our schoolmates' quest for after-school entertainment. We forgot why we were supposed to be angry, and decided to forgo killing each other, since neither of us was willing to risk expulsion from this school. We had only been a part of the progressive education program for a few weeks, and both of us knew that fighting was one of the quickest ways to get us sent back to our old schools, which we both hated. We began to talk. He took a candy bar from his pocket and offered me half—insisting that I take it when I refused. He told me his name, I told him mine, and we walked down the block together. From that day on we were friends.

David's life was as rocky and erratic as mine. From one day to the next he never knew what would become of him. There was no stability at his home, either, and he was sure that if she had someplace to send him, his mother would have done it in a New York minute. He only lived with her because his father was serving a life sentence for murder and the courts had sent David back to her. He told me about it once when we were riding the subway at three in the morning. We did that frequently to get a good night's rest. He was the only person who knew I didn't have a bed and how on countless nights it was impossible to get any sleep at home.

Early in our friendship it became clear that I couldn't lie to him. He was never threatening or judgmental anyway. He just chalked things up to the crummy deals that life threw us. He wasn't ever quick to volunteer information about himself or anyone else, so I didn't worry that people would find out about my life. He began to take charge. David found out which subways had heated cars, and always made sure that he had two tokens. We'd ride the train all night and take turns keeping watch while the other slept. While I was taking refuge from the explosions at my house, David said he was making himself scarce as he was often instructed to do when his mother was entertaining a male guest. Claiming that he wasn't tired, he would often go for hours without waking me. Many were the nights, too, when I bought his convincing story that he could not go home. When I accompanied him back to his house at five or six in the morning, his mother was sleeping—alone—and probably had been all night.

We were always prepared with a story of explanation for any transit cop who questioned us. Sometimes we were going across town because a relative had died, or to get David's little sister, who was lost in Brooklyn. We said "sir" and smiled in all the right places, and we got over. We thanked the cops for their concern, and sometimes they commented about what a pleasure it was to talk to a couple of kids who weren't wise guys.

As everybody knows, the New York transit system isn't the safest place in the world. There were times when we literally had to run for our lives. If it happened to have been a night when a gang was bored and wanted to have some fun on the train, we stayed as inconspicuous as we could, then got off at the next stop and ran like hell. We avoided screwballs and muggers in a variety of different ways. Once, when a seedy bunch looked as though they were going to give us a rough time, I pretended that I was having a seizure while David feigned having a hard time controlling me and asked for help. They took off fast. We followed a particular system depending upon what night of the week it was, because we wanted to make sure that no well-meaning nuisance decided he or she had to help us. We usually alternated our train locations so as not to be recognized easily. As I look back, I realize that we must have had rocks in our heads to expose ourselves to the dangers of isolated plat-forms and deserted cars. Pop always says that God protects drunks and fools. We weren't drunk.

"David Senior," as David sarcastically referred to his father, was an auto mechanic from At-lanta. He had been married several times, and David's mother, who was about ten years younger than his father, was a diversion between wives. He became involved with drugs while in New York, and thought that the money he made deal-ing would far surpass what he earned by getting axle grease all over his hands. By that time he had split up with David's mother, and she sent David to live with him. She said that he was better off being raised by a man, but to hear David tell it, a kid cramped her style and she didn't want to be saddled with one. One evening at his father's house, a fight broke out over a drug sale. David, five years old and shaking in his boots, witnessed it all—"in Technicolor," was the way he worded it. The only details he could recall clearly were the deafening noise that made him cover his ears with his hands, and the sight of blood splattering all over the place. His father fled to escape the police, overlooking the fact that he had left David behind. The day after the drug fight, when the apartment was being investigated for more drugs on the premises, a policeman pulled David from the closet. He was afraid and hungry—and he thought he was dead. It took two hours before he would say a word, five before they were able to contact his mother. Within a few weeks, David Senior was caught, found guilty, and sent to Rikers Island. David told me that he didn't care one way or another. He said that the day of the fight was the day his childhood died, because after that, Mother Goose just couldn't cut it. It was no wonder he always despised shooting and horror movies. Loud noises unnerved him, and blood made him shake in terror.

His most vivid memory of his father was the time the two of them went swimming and his father threw him off a diving board into ten feet of water to teach him how to swim. He was three years old, and when he cried from fright after

someone fished him out, his father called him a
big sissy and threatened to buy him a skirt. David
would watch as his father got high, prepared
drugs for sale, and messed around with women.
"He wasn't a nice person," David said indiffer-
ently. "He had no limits, and he did anything he
wanted. I'm going to do everything I want to do,
but I'm going to do it in a different way."

I asked David if his father ever treated him
well or acted as though he loved him. David
made faces and slapped me on the side of the
head with the palm of his hand. "Stop talking
that love stuff. It's gonna make you sick. We
don't need it."

We needed it, all right. Both of us did. Perhaps that was why each of us sought to prove to
the other that he didn't.

David's mother was an attractive, well-dressed,
well-kept Puerto Rican woman who spoke virtually no English. I asked David once how she
managed to communicate with his father, and
he answered in the most flippant tone I had ever
heard that some things don't require any talking.
It was never hard to figure out that David resented the hell out of her, too. She took him in,
but always made it clear that he was on his own.
She had no time for babying. He was to get himself to school and attend to his own needs and
comfort. He had no curfew. She made sure there
was food in the house, but she didn't cook him
meals. She saw that David had clothes to wear,
but he had to take care of them, and she gave

him a few bucks once in a while. For doing those things she considered herself a good mother, and she always reminded him that there were people who had less than he did. It made him angry. He felt alone in the world, and he blamed both of his parents for it. His bitterness toward them went so deep that he couldn't verbalize it. He remarked more than once that someone should have told them about condoms. I pointed out if that had happened he might not be here. He smiled and said, "It's not like I'm some kind of love child, I'm just here because they were irresponsible and impulsive."

"So am I, so is half the population," I'd argue. "You don't really believe that everyone in this world was welcome and wanted."

That was a discussion not worth having, because David didn't care about everyone in the world. He only cared that his world was as messed up as it was. There were things that grated on him—like having seven brothers and sisters scattered around and not even knowing their names. "You're supposed to take care of your kids," he'd say. Then he'd sigh and go on, "You're supposed to take a dump once a day too, but obviously something went wrong with that, because Ex-Lax is still in business."

My friend was a hard critic of the world, and we sometimes had heated arguments because I refused to think badly of people or situations. It got on his nerves when I smiled at a song or talked about a movie or a book with a powerful message. After all, who cared? I did all of his book reports for him because he couldn't muster up the drive to talk about themes or plots. He simply didn't care. He said that I was trusting and that someday I would learn that I wasn't going to get out of this world alive. Unlike me, he felt that no matter how well something might have turned out, the ride there wasn't worth it.

I laughed at him. "Let's go into the train station and I'll push you off the tracks." He laughed back, and said that I would take him seriously someday. He understood that I did, in fact, know how rough the world was, but that I chose not to acknowledge it all the time. I explained that I had trouble staying angry over things I had no control over. It took energy that I needed to preserve for those hard times. I was afraid that if I adopted his attitude, I wouldn't have the strength to tolerate what I needed to. As a result, he took it upon himself to protect me.

David knew better than anyone the truth of what I lived. Silently he did everything that he could to get me through things. He often saw to my meals, stuffing me with oranges and bananas and sandwiches that he brought from home, saying that I would do him a favor by eating them because his mother would complain that he hadn't. During lunch he always managed to get extra food on his tray, and he made me eat it. To save my pride, he pretended that he wanted it and then complained that it didn't taste good. When we would buy a pretzel from a pushcart vendor, he always saw to it that I got the bigger piece. On days when we had assembly, he always managed to have an extra white shirt already pressed and ready for me in his locker. On winter mornings his backpack was filled with extra sweatshirts and socks for me to put on. When I rebelled, he said that he didn't need me to get sick because there would be no one to do his term papers.

When I was injured at home, he would work to patch me up. As much as he despised the sight of blood, he was an expert at closing up deep gashes. Once, to make a pressure bandage on my arm, he used his socks. There might be only Scotch tape, masking tape, or paper towels for him to work with, but he'd persist until I wasn't bleeding anymore. He'd stuff aspirins down my throat, and always made sure that we had bottles of them on hand at all times. Sometimes it was his eyes that told me he was with me, other times it was the cursing under his breath, the hostile way he threatened to kill my parents. If no one else in the world loved me, he did.

"How long are you going to let them do this?" he'd ask as we huddled inside a bathroom stall at school. It was the only place sometimes where people wouldn't ask questions. "They're gonna kill you, Tone."

I'd shrug, torn between embarrassment and pain.

"Kill their asses first!" he'd growl through

clenched teeth. "Don't let them get you like this." Then he'd lower his head and our eyes would meet and he'd say, "I'll do it for you."

If I'd given David the least encouragement, he would have done it, too. The rage in his face and the blinding fury in his eyes said that he would do anything for me. He understood, though. As much as he wanted me to be able to get out of my house, he knew that my father would track me down and bring me back to consequences I probably would never have survived. He saw what happened to me the few times I did try to resist or fight back, and he begged me not to do it anymore. He agreed that for the time being my options were few, and he'd do whatever it took to keep me here. Particularly after one of those improvised repair sessions, he'd say, "We'll take care of things, okay, Tone?" Then he would suggest that we do something crazy so I wouldn't realize that I hurt so bad.

Once we took turns jumping on the hoods of parked cars and sang songs. The object of the game was to see if you could get through a whole song without laughing, falling off, or getting caught. He went first and launched into the theme from *Shaft* while gyrating on the hood of a Lincoln Continental. When it was my turn I became Bruce Springsteen, and imitated what I had seen in the "Dancing in the Dark" video while atop a Crown Victoria. The car's owner, who was having dinner in the restaurant across the street, came out and threatened to amputate my legs. Summoning my most sorrowful expression, I apologized, told the man that I didn't know what got into me, and offered to wash the car for him. Luckily, he bought my repenting act and told me to go home and never do such a thing again. I promised respectfully that I wouldn't. David said that I was a piece of work, and we laughed for blocks. No one who saw us would have imagined that there was so much turmoil in our lives.

David loved to eat. Once we shared a whole cake together in the park, digging into it on opposite ends with plastic forks. He was happiest when we could go to a breakfast buffet. There was a place around the corner from his house where on Sundays for $2.99 apiece we could eat all we wanted from nine o'clock to noon. He'd always find a way to get us there.

We sometimes went to Times Square and hung out where the hookers and drag queens walked their beats. We went so often that many of them knew us by name and treated us to hot dogs and pretzels. They cautioned us about which cops would ask questions. When someone propositioned us, they'd tell that person in an off-color way to bug off.

"This really sucks," I'd say to David as we sat on a car and took bets on which of the hookers would get the most johns.

"What sucks?" he'd ask absently. He was too busy being amused with their strategies to get philosophical with me.

"*That* sucks, David." I pointed to the hookers. "You call that living?"

"No," he answered matter-of-factly. "I call it surviving. Nobody said anything about living. They're two different things."

"Don't you want to live, David?"

He pinched himself. "I guess this will have to do for now." That was just a part of his to-hell-with-it attitude. If he took the time to analyze what he didn't like, it made him disheartened and angry.

David wanted to be an engineer and travel all around the world building things. He didn't want to take in art or beauty. All he wanted was to be able to reach into his pocket and pull out money when he wanted to. He wanted a house that he could be comfortable in, a refrigerator filled with food, closets and drawers loaded with choices of clothes. He wanted it to happen now, and he hated that everything he wanted had to be a struggle. He resented the concept of "someday."

David and I were approached several times to be drug dealers in our school and others in our area. The front guys said that we were smart— and what was most ideal was that we didn't look the part. The two of us discussed it at length one night. The good points were obvious. There were kids our age wearing designer clothes and holding leases on their own apartments filled with furniture. We would have had to be push-ers, though—peddling poison and misery to other kids. Neither of us could do that. We knew a few kids who got into trouble because of drugs—good kids who otherwise would have done all right for themselves. We decided to try doing the right thing before resorting to all kinds of low-down measures to get something.

"I'm tempted," David said, "but I never want to hide in a closet again." It wasn't so much a matter of our being honorable; peddling drugs was just more than we could handle. Our consciences ruled us, but we fought them tooth and nail every day because that kind of money and freedom was pretty attractive. Still, we didn't need one more thing to make us hate ourselves.

We decided that we had to make do. Sometimes we wanted to give up, to run off together where nobody could find us. We entertained thoughts of hiding out in the subway tunnels, but neither of us liked dirt or rats. David hated it when I got quiet and read a lot. He knew I needed to escape into another world, and he didn't want me to do that. "Come on, Tone, we'll handle things," he'd assure me. Then we would find something outrageous to do. We would sit on the stoops of apartment buildings and try to outdo each other singing old songs. We waited at the back door of many Broadway shows to see who we could catch coming out. David was the only person in my life who knew who I really was, apart from all of the stories I told to convince everyone else that I was all right. We were hungry together, lonely and tired together, and often afraid together. We never knew what the next day would bring, and it scared us to wonder whether things would get worse. Our saving grace lay in the fact that we were able to tolerate things together. It was an unspoken pact between the two of us that we would take care of each other.

Whenever David and I made plans, we always assumed that whatever life brought one of us, the other would figure into it. We were to meet at midnight on December 31, 2027, and toast our fiftieth year on earth. The best-laid plans . . .

# Zeke

He walked with a limp, and his horn-rimmed glasses were as thick as Coke bottles. He stuttered, and often paused in midsentence to regroup his thoughts. When we played cards, he counted them out in groups of three and pronounced the word *tree*. He couldn't tell you when his birthday was unless he looked in his wallet at his union ID card. He had to think about it before he could name the current president, although he remembered clearly the day that JFK "bought it." The only thing he did with newspapers was check the daily number—always commenting how close or far away he was from "hitting it big." He never figured that he would win. We met because I passed his building every day on the way to school. We always smiled and waved and we asked each other questions. If it was after school and the ice-cream truck was parked outside, he'd call to me and get one for both of us. From our many conversations, consisting mostly of his selective memories, I learned that his education was limited to junior high school. On his own since he was sixteen, he declared that his job as porter and doorman of this apartment building was the best job of his thirty-nine years. His makeshift apartment—a storeroom in the building's basement—was a castle to him.

The building superintendent called him a kindhearted simpleton. Tenants took turns giving him leftovers from each night's supper. Bob, the handyman, brought him sacks of clothes that he no longer wanted. Zeke tore into them as if he had just come from shopping at Macy's. His bed was two unmatched mattresses that someone had tossed out onto the sidewalk. He turned them in such a way that the springs would not poke him, and pronounced them as good as new. His pillow was a laundry sack stuffed with old clothes. He watched TV—mostly reruns of old shows—on a sixteen-inch black and white set that he rescued from the garbage. Most of the time he could only pick up three channels. His transistor radio had a piece of coat hanger that served as an antenna. Zeke's world and all that he cared about was this building on West 84th Street.

I was crazy about Zeke. He didn't know—or care a damn—about schoolwork, the honor roll, or my troubles at home. He was just happy to play with me because it was fun. Many were the nights I sat opposite him on a milk crate in the lobby, having a terrific time. He taught me how to blow bubble gum, and always had a fresh piece in his pocket. He instructed me on the proper way to flip baseball cards, and taught me how to play checkers with a set that he retrieved from a trash bag. On Saturday nights, Zeke, his radio, and I were tuned in to the doo-wop show on WCBS. He taught me how to harmonize a cappella, and said that the bathroom was the best place for a good sound. It was Zeke who suggested that I flip my hair up in the front, and I've been doing it ever since. I was forever snapping my fingers and singing "Runaround Sue." When the goings-on at home were too much to contend with, I'd find Zeke sitting on a box in front of the building. With him I had the luxury of being a child. I could do things that made no sense to anyone but me.

On Thursdays and Saturdays I accompanied Zeke as he drove the service elevator from floor to floor and pulled in the building's garbage. Unlike the one the tenants used, this elevator had a lever on the side with an up-and-down control on it that looked like a large joystick. Zeke hardly ever pulled the metal safety gate in front of us, and with the air hitting us in the face, it felt as if we were flying. He let me drive it as he sifted through the refuse. Almost always he came upon lamps, books, sometimes expensive clothing. He cleaned up a Mickey Mouse watch that was stuffed at the bottom of a sack and gave it to me. Everything was a treasure and served a useful purpose. It bothered him that people threw things away instead of cleaning them or fixing them up. It was a blast, too, to throw large plastic sacks into the trash room and listen to their contents crashing against one another. And the whole time we belted out "Big Girls Don't Cry," or one of my favorites, "The Wanderer."

One morning when I was headed for school, I met Zeke in our usual spot in the lobby. Before I could tell him that I had heard a Four Seasons hour the night before on the radio, he told me that we needed to say good-bye. His job was being taken over by a younger man who could get around better. In one breath I asked why he didn't complain to the union representative, where he would go, and whether we would see each other again. To each question he shook his head and smiled. His simple words said that we'd probably never see each other again, and he was willing to take this in his stride. He said he'd always remember me. I gave him my Mickey Mouse watch to make sure he really would remember me. I wanted to tell him how much I'd miss him, that he was a great friend, but I bolted from the building and ran all the way to school.

Was this it? You just waved good-bye to someone you'd shared so many good times with? I couldn't get it straight in my head. Uncooperative in school that whole day, I defied someone to challenge me. Enraged, I wondered how much younger a man needed to be to pull garbage. It was all crazy and very unfair, so I convinced myself not to miss Zeke and to learn to cope as well as he did when things were rotten.

Some three years later, in a subway station, I heard someone calling my name. I turned to see a pathetic figure huddled in a corner against a wall. I stood before him apprehensively. "Did you call me?" I asked.

Stuttering, he asked whether I remembered him. I studied his features, and they slowly came into focus. The thick eyeglasses were taped at the rims. His right leg had been amputated at the knee.

"Zeke, is that you?"

He nodded and lifted his dirty sleeve to expose the Mickey Mouse watch. I smiled, but was deeply saddened. He seemed like a rag of what I remembered. He told me how he'd been forced out of his apartment and put out on the street when the building went co-op. Because of his disability, he was ineligible to stay in homeless shelters. Hospitals claimed that he was not sick enough to be admitted. He survived by panhandling, occasionally sleeping in a friend's basement, or hanging out in the train stations until the police threw him out.

I stared at Zeke. A half-eaten pretzel that he was saving for later lay on top of a newspaper next to him. He offered it to me—a gesture that brought a lump to my throat. It was always this way. Those who had nothing would give you everything wholeheartedly—those who were overflowing with things that they didn't need never had enough and always made excuses. I handed Zeke the fifty cents I was saving and the Walkman that I had won in the school spelling bee. He thanked me and told me to look for him again whenever I rode the train.

I kicked a can into the tracks as I thought of that stupid request of Mayor Koch's that we not give to panhandlers. His distorted reasoning was that we could aid people like Zeke by contributing to the various shelters throughout the city. It only goes to show that he and those like him in this richest and most elite city in the world know nothing about the many Zekes out there—about what it feels like to lose your job to a younger man. I question those who state that people are homeless because they want to be. I don't believe that's always the case. I saw a man asleep standing in a doorway and all I could think about was the fact that he must want to survive pretty badly to tolerate this. Think about how you feel if, as an overnight guest, you are made to sleep on someone's couch. Pretty inconvenient, right? How sleepy you must be to sprawl out on the ground under a box, on a park bench, or underneath the subway tracks, where rats fight you for territory. I knew the feeling all too well. Turning away doesn't work. That nagging indigence and those blank expressions are still going to be there—regardless of our dismay and uncomfortable reactions. There's got to be more we can do than work in a soup kitchen or donate clothes to Goodwill to make space in our closets. While the homeless are unpleasant to look at, they are a frightening reminder that this can happen to us.

I told Zeke to take care of himself and immediately wanted to kick myself for sounding so condescending. I didn't shake his hand or kiss him—I didn't want to. I turned away quickly so that our eyes wouldn't meet. Perhaps Zeke was better off in many ways than I was. He asked no questions, placed no blame. Things were what they were. That, too, was frightening. What would become of me in years to come if at this age I was sleeping in the subway? Would my temperament allow me to be as complacent as Zeke? I truly doubted it. I knew that I would have to do something about my situation or die. I got on the train, blew a bubble with my gum, and exhaustion overcame me. I decided to sleep. I hoped that Zeke would sleep too.

# Me and P.G.

I remember those ridiculous classroom assignments to write a paper about "How I Spent My Summer Vacation." They were idiotic, and I always made up elaborate summer adventures to suit my teachers and earn myself a good grade. One year I went water skiing in Florida, the next I camped in the mountains. I learned early on that it was to my benefit to start the school year off on the right foot. Teachers assume a whole lot—reasoning that if a student is in a progressive program, he has a privileged home life. Not always—not most of us. Therefore it was easy for me to go on for pages about things that never happened. I'd give a little geography lesson—compliments of the encyclopedia—and throw in a pinch of learning experiences, and that would win me congratulations and passage into my gullible teachers' good graces. Charlotte, the spider in *Charlotte's Web*, knew what she was talking about when she said that humans were gullible, that they believed anything they saw in print. My teachers were living testimony to that. The problem was that the more I lied, the more desperate I felt about the truth of the situation that I lived in.

Also on the list of horrid composition assignments were "The Person I Most Admire" and "My Plans for the Future." Ruben, a guy in sixth grade, was nearly expelled because he wrote about how he'd like to become a pimp, because pimping would be a profitable enterprise and it would be the best and easiest way to connect with beautiful girls. He saw it as a great move out of a miserable ghetto existence. Teachers who lived in the suburbs—and even those who didn't, but who lived fairly decently—seldom comprehended that there is often no place for morality or integrity when you are trying to escape such misery. What was sad—almost scary—was that Ruben got into trouble because he told the truth. No one grasped that truth for the depth that it held.

It got so that these tasks exhausted me. I didn't want to write compositions anymore, because they were born of my wishful thinking. It didn't feel good that my teachers were praising the biggest conglomeration of fiction that I could come up with. They didn't want to know it was fiction, either. The reality was that I had no summer vacations to speak of. I didn't admire anyone worthy of writing about, and I was so consumed in the present that I couldn't be bothered to enlist the energy to write about a future that seemed light-years away. I wanted a future, but the here and now was always so overwhelming. Maybe if someone had encouraged me to write the truth, it would have worked for me. I would have had plenty to say—my heart would have gone into it. I would have been proud of myself. They never asked for that, though. So I lied— lied through my teeth and hated myself because I was being showered with praise for it.

The year I entered Mr. Blume's class and he asked for a five-hundred-word composition about a valuable relationship, I was ready to take a zero before agreeing to write another fictitious essay. Sure, I could have had an imaginary uncle or a wise former teacher up my sleeve to rave about, but I didn't want to lie again. So I told the truth in an unexpected way. My stubbornness earned me a C and some merciless teasing from fellow classmates when Mr. Blume read my work aloud and acted as if it were the most farfetched and moronic story he had ever heard. So be it. It was the first honest piece I had ever written. Mr. Blume contended that my "valuable relationship" lesson was best learned by kindergartners, not relatively intelligent students in an honors class. He didn't care that this relationship had taught me so much about myself because it had helped me understand limitations and how we can only take as much as can honestly be given. He wasn't interested that I learned that such honesty could fulfill me.

The lesson I learned, you see, was from a gray striped cat that lived in the back alley of my tenement building. I happened upon her one afternoon as I sat out there on a discarded milk crate with a slice of pizza, looking for a place to escape. I thought I could buy some peace before it was time to go home to whatever disaster was imminent. It had been a horrible day. My body was sore, I was tired, and as a punishment for crying when my father hit me, I was not going to be allowed to eat for the rest of the week. I felt hopeless about everything and I was about at the end of my rope. The owner of the pizzeria around the block had given me a free slice of pizza and a can of Pepsi because I took a package to the post office for him. I had no idea what mood my father would be in, but I knew how he'd react to my accepting food, so the back alley seemed a good place to steal a few minutes of solitude. The pizza was good. As I bit into it, I realized that I was truly hungry. I hadn't been eating very much because withholding food was the punishment my parents were using against me lately, and I suddenly felt very sorry for myself because of it. I leaned against the window and closed my eyes, chewing each bite many times to make the pizza last.

The loud *meow* roused me from my reverie—it was strong and persistent, so I opened my eyes and looked at her. She was kind of cute and obviously pregnant. The sac underneath her seemed much too big for her tiny frame. Her large green eyes were on my pizza as she continued for a minute or so with that steady *meow*. I ripped a small piece from my slice and held it out to her. Strangely, she backed away.

"Suit yourself," I mumbled as I threw it on the ground, frustrated for not knowing what she wanted. She immediately pounced on it, devouring it in less than thirty seconds. "Now why would you want to eat off the ground?" I asked as I threw another piece that she immediately seized. I laughed, and for the next few minutes I alternated bites between the two of us. I'd take a bite and then throw another down, continuing until there wasn't any left. Then she sat and licked her front paws, and as I bent over to pet her, she moved away, jumping up abruptly and running into a small hole in the building wall across the way. "You're very welcome!" I called out to her as I picked up my can of Pepsi and started to leave. My mood had lightened. I was smiling as I headed home.

The next day I thought about her and that huge belly. I wondered if she had enough to eat. Waiting until the kids tore out into the schoolyard, I stayed behind in the lunchroom and scrounged through the trash for throwaways from lunches. I put bits and pieces of cold cuts and bread together in a little plastic bag and hoped that no one would come in and see me. I shuddered at the thought that anyone might think I was doing this for myself.

After school, I ran all the way to the back alley. Maybe she'd be around again. Perhaps this time she'd let me pick her up and pet her.

"P.G.," I called out. The name came from Whoopi Goldberg's impression of a pregnant valley girl, in which she describes her condition by saying she is "totally P.G." "Come on out." I gave a shrill, loud whistle and she finally popped her head through the hole and came out toward me—half stalking, half swaggering. I admired her cocky attitude. "Nice of you to come out," I kidded. "You like pizza so much, let's see what you think of bologna." Again I held out a piece in front of her—and, as the day before, she backed away. "Have it your way, dirt merchant," I said, scowling as if she could really be offended, and dropped a scrap on the ground. Just as she had done the day before, she pounced on it. I fed her the rest of the pieces one by one, watching as she devoured each one hungrily. She stared up at me when I took too long to throw any more down.

I watched as she ate furiously for the next few minutes, envying her ease in accepting what I tossed away. She wasn't at all bothered that I knew she wanted it. Her stomach would be in better shape than mine tonight.

Maybe this cat knew something I didn't. She cared nothing about saving face. What did she know about embarrassment or humiliation? I would starve to death before I'd ever acknowledge to anyone that I was hungry. I always wanted to throw a rock or something at those kids at school who thought nothing of begging for free boxes of cereal that the teacher told them to take "only if they were needy." They were just like P.G., pouncing on the food with no regard for appearances. I realized that I had no right to be angry with them. My hang-ups—and I had plenty—should not have been pushed on them. I bit my tongue more than once to keep from telling them to shove their needy people's food so far up that it would come out the other end. I got chills when announcements came over the PA system during Thanksgiving week, somewhere between the Pledge of Allegiance and the passing up of lunch forms: "Anyone wishing consideration for the limited Thanksgiving baskets, come to the office now and leave your name." I would die of starvation first. I'm not saying, either, that this fierce and stubborn pride within me is right. It's probably downright stupid. I know, though, that I won't do anything but clutch at it with all I have and hold it as tight as I can—whatever the cost. It serves me because I am able to show through my presence alone that I have survived in spite of what has not been done for me. I guess, too, that I preferred to die of starvation than of embarrassment.

Ironically, this distorted sense of self-consciousness was precisely the reason that I took it upon myself to feed P.G. I could make that possible, at least. Even if I didn't eat that day, she wouldn't go hungry, and so, in my own twisted way, I was securing my own survival. My goal was to take care of her and her unborn kittens—an unsuspecting litter that would, no doubt, go through the same trouble, the same hunger, and the same perpetuation of misery, into another generation. I wondered often about my own enthusiasm, but continued to give in to it. It made me feel alive and vital.

As weeks passed, I made my daily visits to the back alley with the lunch scraps. Sometimes I managed to find a milk carton or two. P.G. had begun to respond to her name. I loved the way she would run from the hole when she heard it. It was as if we had a secret code—yes, strange as it was, we had a relationship. I would go through my ritual of scattering the scraps on the ground, and then would watch intently until she ate the last one. Sometimes she would walk between my legs and purr—and sometimes she only sat and stared at me. I would talk to her and she seemed to listen. I couldn't touch her, though, and each time I tried, she bolted and ran back into her hole.

"You could ask once in a while if I needed some company," I'd sigh, wishing she would stay a few more minutes. She wouldn't, though, and she didn't consider whether or not she had hurt my feelings. P.G. was being real. She was staying true to herself. It was the first time I truly understood such a concept. I saw so often that people took such pains with protocol and "doing the right thing," which wasn't always right anyway. P.G.'s sense of "the right thing" was what she felt. She didn't understand hypocrisy or "have to"s. There had to be something to that.

Then for two weeks when I went to the back alley, P.G. didn't come out. I would wait two or three hours, then scatter the food and leave, feeling lonely and rejected. I missed her. I had come to depend upon those moments we shared. I was so proud that I had been the one to care for her. Her not coming out made me angry. She seemed so disloyal. She never, even in thanks, let me pet her. She never said good-bye.

I sat on my milk crate, wanting to kick myself for getting so emotional over a pea-brained cat. It became obvious that maybe I needed her more than she needed me. I got up and looked over inside her hole again. I jumped as a rat scurried past me and made its way up an adjoining fire escape.

"P.G., won't you *please* come out?" I begged. She didn't.

I threw the bag of food on the ground. Who did she think she was, anyway? I didn't owe her anything! Not companionship, not compassion, not a meal. That was when things became clear. *No, I didn't.* P.G. asked, and *I* opted to respond. Yes, she was the beneficiary of all my efforts, but they were my choice from the start and not hers. I was doing what *I* wanted to do. That was how people got into trouble. They got mad because other people didn't respond to their actions. Such situations in my life came into clear focus. Giving, sharing, friendship, and—the biggest of all—love cannot be orchestrated; to do so would dilute the purity of their worth. They've got to be spontaneous, no matter what the outcome. I decided then and there that I preferred honesty. It would make me know that gestures were sincere, that love was real. I didn't want them otherwise.

A few days later, when I sat on my milk crate and leaned against the wall, P.G. reemerged from the hole.

"P.G.!" I shouted. "Where have you been?" I took the bag from my pocket and threw a piece of ham on the ground. She ate it and, just as suddenly as she had surfaced, disappeared into the hole again. As I called her name and tried to coax her with food, her head popped through the hole, and this time there was something in her mouth. Just what I need, I thought. Her prize catch of the day. She placed it on the ground, looked up at me, and meowed. It was a kitten! I bent down to stroke its head, and as I did so, she walked in and out between my legs and meowed. Then she went back into the hole twice more, and brought the remaining two kittens out. I stroked and petted them for a few minutes, smiling and contented. Here we were, in a back alley in the middle of the Upper West Side, and the signs of beauty were all around us. Right before me—life and its very simple wonders—were the reasons for struggle. P.G. didn't know it, but she was sharing with me what was precious to her. I was honored. Tenderness could be felt under *any* terms as long as it was sincere. I immediately named the kittens Mantle, Gehrig, and DiMaggio.

I continued to make daily trips to the back alley and saw to the meals for my family of four. I never even shared the secret of the cats with David, because this small world was mine, and it was perfect. Even the kittens came to know my whistle. Gehrig willingly ate from my hand and climbed on me. It became increasingly harder to say good-bye.

One afternoon when I got out of school, I headed for my spot, but the handyman stopped me and told me not to go into the alley.

"Why not?"

"You wouldn't want to," he said. "There are a bunch of dead cats back there. We're waiting for the city to come and clean it up."

I couldn't believe it. "What happened?" I asked.

He said that some cats had gotten into the building and someone had been feeding them. He made a face and waved his hand in the direction of the alley. "They got rid of them." He told me my own father had done the landlord the favor and shot them.

*Got rid of them.* Those words were so much a part of my world. That's just what was always done when it came to anything or *anyone* that got in the way. Who knew when it would be my turn? I took the cold cuts and milk cartons from my pocket and dumped them on the street as I headed upstairs. I was so afraid and I felt so alone. I didn't understand why life had to be so filled with apprehension and dread. Would it ever change, or would I end up dying afraid? How long would the threat hang over my head that someone might get rid of me? I didn't cry on the way to the apartment or when I got there, either. I just waited for my stomach to settle and started on my homework. It seemed the only thing to do.

# The Rescue

There were mice in the school basement. An eccentric art teacher who ate broccoli sandwiches and called Vincent Van Gogh her hero happened upon one while searching for supplies and screamed loud enough to make everyone think she was being attacked by the Boston Strangler. As she sat in the nurse's office with cold compresses on her forehead, she described the mouse as if it were a descendant of Willard and Ben. She contended that if that fiendish animal had the audacity to show itself in broad daylight, then its family had to be close by.

For the next two days the mice were the chief topic of conversation in every classroom, at every lunch table, and even in the hallways and bathrooms. Each time the story circulated, the mice became more and more ferocious. Never mind the favorable publicity that rodents received in the movie *An American Tail*. After all of this frightening talk, no one could envision a cute and cuddly Fievel Mousekewitz. The panic intimated that bubonic plague was imminent.

In an effort to quiet the hysteria, the principal ordered the custodian to place a dozen or so traps in the basement to do the pests in. While this action appeased the excitable art teacher, who was blowing air into a paper sack to keep from hyperventilating, my friend Allison went into a lather of her own. She was appalled at this cold-blooded sentence.

You had to know Allison. At first glance she could easily be seen as a candidate for the Bizarre Hall of Fame. An avowed vegetarian because she refused to eat anything at the expense of a murdered animal, at age twelve Allison belonged to all sorts of humane organizations and committees. She drew up petitions against fur coat manufacturers, and God help anyone who came to school with a cheap rabbit fur coat or a leather jacket; they were guaranteed a forty-five-minute lecture on the evils of trapping. Tearfully she'd recount the horrible pain that an unsuspecting, innocent animal had to endure just because someone wanted to wear a fur coat. She organized protests in our school to end unnecessary dissections in biology classes. David, our friend Joey, and I had to intercede a few times when fights would break out and people would want to bash her face in.

I liked Allison, though—actually, I loved her. She was cheerful and upbeat, the youngest of three children. Her siblings were grown and out of the house, and her parents, both prominent attorneys, were often busy with work or social commitments. Housekeepers usually attended to her needs. Once we had taken a very complicated history exam. No one got better than a sixty-five, and we were upset about it because it meant four more weeks with that teacher. Knowing that there wasn't a damn thing we could do about it, Allison organized a "let's celebrate" party and we went to the park to play kickball. She was a gentle person, loving and vulnerable and extremely aware of what people were thinking or feeling, without their saying a word. It bothered her when someone was sad, and it made her angry when a person was made a scapegoat. When the question came up once of whether abortion should be legal, she sympathized for the unborn fetus—cried, as a matter of fact—but changed her opinion when she heard about what some women went through on account of unwanted pregnancies. She knew sometimes that I wasn't in the best of moods because of reasons that escaped her. I never talked about home. She left Pepsi cans in my locker with smiley faces scrawled across them and "Have a nice day" written underneath. It was a treat to watch her take apart a poem or draw a picture. She was a person I thought for sure would grow up to be world-famous.

Flushed, wide-eyed, and impatient, Allison caught up to David and me in the music lab and motioned for us to follow her. She had already yanked Joey—her "best friend in the whole world"—from a history class by pretending to deliver a message to the office. He shrugged behind her back at our questioning glances as she led us to the back staircase and down to the basement. Halfway down, David stopped in his tracks and said, "What are we doing here? We don't have a hall pass."

"Did you hear about the mousetraps?" Allison asked in a panic-filled voice. "If it weren't for that broccoli-eating jerk, those animals would be living in peace."

David stared at her in disbelief. "This is about those traps in the basement?" She nodded and he made a face. "C'mon, Allison, what's wrong with a dozen less mice in New York City? Get rid of those and we still have too many." He wouldn't let her protest. "They're rodents, Alli— they breed all kinds of diseases and carry rabies. They'd bite you in a heartbeat, too. They don't care that you're crazy enough to risk your butt to save them. Let's get the hell back to class before we get caught down here."

Leave it to David to be practical. He saw no point in getting into trouble—or troubling himself—because there were very few things worth that effort to him.

Allison wasn't budging. "People carry and spread diseases too," she argued. "No one judges them or puts out traps to catch them. They find doctors, hire research teams that look for cures. Who are we to say that *they* don't have the right?"

"They," David argued back, "are mice. I can't believe we're even here having this conversation."

That was when Allison started proclaiming the merits of life and everyone's lack of regard for it. Choking back giggles, Joey got on his knees and swore that he was into life. There was very little that Joey took seriously. He was always ready to go along with the program at hand, and he could find humor in just about anything. Allison was always telling him to take things more seriously, but eventually she wound up giggling at him. He could do that to her. Not this time, though—she was on a steady roll. So was he. He and David broke into the famous "L'Chaim" routine from *Fiddler on the Roof.* I, too, had begun to laugh with them until I noticed tears streaming down her face.

"C'mon, Alli, cut it out," I urged. "They're just kidding. Don't turn this into a life-or-death issue."

"That's what it is!" she shouted. "This is not about levels of life or even what we would call quality. It's just about life. Period!" David, Joey, and I glanced at one another, then at Allison. I leaned against the wall with my arms crossed, stunned that I was making sense of her argument when what I really wanted to do was laugh. That was so much less complicated than having to evaluate life's worth. At that point I was on fast forward and almost dared not to do it for fear that I'd scare myself with an honest response. We were saving mice and I wasn't sure if I could save myself.

Allison sat down on a crate and wiped her eyes on her sleeve. "I know that everyone thinks I'm crazy." She paused for a second and then said between sobs, "I'm 'Wacko Alli,' who won't step on a roach or swat a fly, right? I know what everyone says behind my back." We didn't answer, and she went on, "It just occurs to me that we place our priorities on everything. Why should we? What right have *we* got to decide that those mice should be trapped and killed? Who the hell do we think we are that we're entitled to make all the decisions?" By this time she was outraged and we were paying attention. "We're supposed to be the ones of superior intelligence—maybe we need to give that lots of thought. Did you ever wonder what happens— even to a mouse—during that split second between life and death? Maybe someone can step in to stop it. Maybe mice deserve it too."

Suddenly David became angry. "No one escapes without dying, Allison. It doesn't matter how many petitions you sign or how many organizations you belong to. Death is something that we never beat. Those mice that you're crying about are going to die one way or another. If not a mousetrap, then maybe a big fat cat—or just plain old age."

The bitterness of his tone frightened me. For as much and as long as I had known David, I'd never realized how defeated he felt. "So are we.

No matter how much medical technology tempts it—we're going!"

"That's okay if it's natural," Allison argued back. "People and animals die every minute of every day. Some say that the process is even beautiful—but it's got to happen when it's supposed to. Things like mousetraps and fly swatters, roach poison, guns, knives, grenades—nuclear bombs! We just keep going up another level. They're all a bully's way of beating something smaller. Why do there always have to be winners and losers? Why do the strong always have to overpower the weak? The worst wouldn't be that those mice died, but that they got caught in those traps and didn't know why." She looked at us, begging again for understanding. "The very worst thing would be if they got caught in those traps and *didn't* die. Have you got any idea what it feels like to be trapped?"

David looked at me and I swallowed hard. I turned away because I didn't want him to decipher my thoughts. Since she had put it that way, I had to admit that she wasn't wrong.

It was obvious that this had to do with plenty more than mice. It had to do with *us*—with a position, a point of view. David threw his hands up in the air and then slapped them on his hips. "Let's get this over with."

For the next half hour we worked to remove the traps, snapping them shut with mop handles. Then we threw them in the back of a large storage cabinet. Joey began to call to the mice, shouting that the war was over and they were free. We laughed, but then stopped and stared at one another. They *were* free. Like it or not, we'd all shared in this impetuous burst of energy. Our act was about nothing more than preserving life—not any specific kind or quality, but just life. We had long forgotten to respect its meaning, but for the first time in ages we'd taken a stand.

When we were asked to account for the hour that we were missing, we made up an excuse about a biology research project and were lucky because the teachers were in no mood to question us. In more ways than one we got over.

That night, as I stared out at the traffic in the street, I thought about many things. No one changes the world. For all of Allison's crusading, there was always going to be someone to challenge her. Mousetraps were still going to be used; we still had access to guns, knives, and nuclear bombs. Diseases were a means of financing sports cars for cocky physicians who thought they had the world by the short hairs by virtue of their prescription pads. Therefore I didn't fool myself into believing that our attack in the basement would be an act that would go down in history. Still, life *was*—there was no more to it than that—and *that* was good.

# Fantasy

When I was six, story hour in Mrs. McNeil's first-grade class was my favorite part of the day. It was a chance to get away from thick, bulky pencils and puzzle-page books—not to mention a confining desk. It meant that the rest of the day would be smooth sailing. I sat on a mat in the middle of the floor, transfixed by my teacher's thick Irish brogue as she read stories about handsome princes who rescued poor, victimized maidens like Cinderella. The stories were very predictable. The prince usually fell in love—at first sight, of course—and he always managed to win his maiden over by rescuing her from a horrible situation or waking her from a deathlike sleep with a kiss. They'd go riding off into the sunset where they lived happily ever after atop a mountain where they woke to the sound of chirping birds. Happily ever after—what a great idea!

For years, teachers and parents have been reading to starry-eyed kids about the wonders of fairy-tale lives. Every little girl wants to be the beautiful princess, every little boy wants to ride off into the sunset with the sweetest girl he ever laid eyes on. The truth is—and it comes through very quickly—that happily ever after is a sick joke. No one lived that way, and it made me angry that such ideas and expectations could be planted in children's minds. It made me angrier yet that wonderful things and feelings were always make-believe. Everyone isn't prince or princess material. Real situations and circumstances usually bear no resemblance to Paradise or magic.

I almost believed this fantasy—for about half a minute. Story hour ended, though, and I would head back to my seat wistfully. I knew well that what I had just experienced—and enjoyed so very much—was just a story. After all, such romantic discoveries never took place in New York City. I couldn't think of anyone who would be willing to rescue me. I couldn't imagine ever being able to get away from where I was. That was the difference between reality and make-believe. In real life there were seldom happy endings.

As I grew older, I became more disillusioned—and less inclined to devote a great deal of myself to happily-ever-afters. They made me crazy, and my immediate existence held no place for them. I had no desire for a life that resembled a Disney musical. I developed an apathetic indifference to sentiment—sap, as I called it. I understood all too well that in real life, Cinderella kept her pretty but sad self home and scrubbed those dirty floors—got knocked on the head with a two-by-four if she didn't. Her confidence was deflated and she was told that there would be no ball for her—that her sorry butt wasn't going anywhere. The only prince that she would ever know would be a do-nothing, know-nothing in search of some momentary pleasure. He'd leave after having his own way—while making her think that it was just what she wanted. Pretty funny, right? Not really. It's very sad. My class was filled with Cinderellas and Prince Charmings who invested valuable energy and spirit in the promise of that idyllic fantasy. Many were second-generation welfare kids—some didn't even know who their own fathers were. Some were well on their way to perpetuating this cycle in search of happily-ever-after.

Then Jessie happened. She wore her dark hair very long in the back and feathered in the front. She was much more sophisticated and mature than the other girls in my class who were eleven years old. She wore makeup and a bra that she didn't stuff. She acted worldly—very experienced. Hence she became a distracting fascination to most of the guys. The girls, on the other hand, hated her. As luck would have it, she took a shine to me during rehearsals for a drama club musical number called *Fantasy*, in which I got involved because it got me excused from a few classes and it would earn me a good grade for my drama class. Jessie began to smile at me, and I'd smile back. Then she cut through the other girls to be my partner. She stood next to me and held my hand during curtain calls. I can't say I didn't enjoy the attention.

From the get-go, guys were congratulating me, whispering "She puts out," every opportunity they got. Tim cornered me in the bathroom.

"Who's the luckiest son of a bitch in this school?" He patted my back like a proud father.

"I don't know, who is?"

"I guess you can afford to be smug. I've been trying to get into her pants for two months. She's practically giving them away to you."

The statement offended me—I couldn't figure out why—and it showed on my face. Tim assumed it was because he was nosing into my business, so he apologized. "Look, Tony. She's crazy about you and I'm jealous."

"Did she tell you that?"

"No, but it couldn't get any more obvious. You're in business! We're going on that trip to Pennsylvania Dutch Country. Did you forget it's an overnighter?"

I waved him away, hoping my embarrassment didn't show. I'd never been as happy or relieved when the bell rang.

I sat, half listening to a lecture about the Declaration of Independence. I was filled with confusing thoughts—definitely curious about all of these issues I knew very little about. Jessie turned sideways and winked at me. Of course Tim noticed. He gave me a thumbs-up sign. I tore a page from my notebook and tried to be as charming as possible as I wrote, "How about a walk in Central Park after school? The pretzels are on me."

She turned around again. Her smile served as a response.

Before the day was out, word had circulated that Jessie and I had an official "date." The ribbing began. David, for one, was merciless.

"Hey, Tone, I'm jealous. Can I be the first to congratulate you?"

I gave him a dirty look. "Yeah, and while you're at it, cough up a couple of bucks for me."

"I get it," he teased. "Paying for services?"

"No—actually for pretzels."

He took two dollars from his pocket and handed them to me with his familiar scowl. "You're getting off easy."

I was losing my temper with everyone, and I took it out on David. "This is getting on my nerves already. I mean it."

David made a face and started to walk away, then turned back again. He stared at me angrily. "That's just like you, Tony."

"What's just like me?"

"To act like you couldn't care less when you know that competition is fierce for her attention."

"Why is that, David?"

"Use your imagination," he answered impatiently. "She provides a service that everyone's interested in—I guess except you. You want to buy pretzels."

"What do you want me to do? Take her up on some roof and do the nasty?"

He shrugged. "Rumor has it that she'll do it without too much fight."

That was when Jessie came out of the building. We both said hello and I glared at David. This was all going too fast for me. Yes, we were smart—we threw that fact up every chance we got to whoever would listen—but we were still not yet twelve years old. If I started heading for rooftops—doing things that I didn't have a clue about how to begin to do—what would I have to look forward to when I was sixteen? Besides, at that point in my life, sex held no appeal for me. I decided then and there to approach Jessie in a different way. We took that walk through Central Park and shared a pretzel—and we talked. I learned that blue was her favorite color, that gardenias were her favorite flowers—she'd seen *Lady Sings the Blues*, and said they were romantic. She had read the Bible from cover to cover and was memorizing the Psalms because they comforted her when she was afraid. In the past year her father had deserted the family, her older sister had overdosed on crack, and her mother had been through three different boyfriends. Contrary to what my friends tried to get me to believe, "Jessie the nympho" was just as scared and vulnerable as the rest of us.

The weight of peer pressure crowded in a few weeks later when we got to the hotel in Pennsylvania Dutch Country. The guys were determined that this would be my night. Jessie heard about it and agreed with them. She showed up in my room after bed check, looking prettier than usual. She sat down next to me on the bed and smiled. I smiled back.

"So where do you want to do it?" she asked as she began to rub my chest and go lower.

I sat up. "Just a second. I have to ask you something." She nodded and I continued. "Do you always make it so easy for guys to get their way with you?"

There wasn't an ounce of hesitation. "Sure, why not?"

I was angry and exasperated for her. "You're so pretty—that's why not! Why do you make yourself so cheap?"

She stood up, and for a minute I thought she would slap my face. Her eyes brimmed with tears. "*What* did you say?"

"Jessie, why do you work so hard at being easy?"

"You're here with me, aren't you? You must want something."

Her accusing tone annoyed me. "I like you," I stated as evenly as I could. "If I want someone to make out with, I'll let you know."

Jessie nodded her head and sat down. "Are you gay, Tony?"

"I don't want to paw you like a leopard, so that means I'm gay? You really think the world of yourself, don't you?"

"Come on," she said softly. "Don't get mad at me, I like you."

"I like you, too."

She seemed shocked. "You do?"

"Why the hell do you think I talk to you—that I'm here with you in the first place?"

"I thought—"

"Well, you thought wrong. We're eleven years old and it scares me to pretend that we should be doing things that we've got no business doing yet."

"Everybody does it, Tony."

I made a disapproving face. "Everyone *says* they do it."

Jessie began to cry, and I became afraid. "Please don't do that," I implored. I shouldn't have said that, either—shouldn't have told her not to cry. Perhaps the very thing that made her so sad was the reason that she was willing to compromise herself so much. I didn't understand how important it was to let yourself feel whatever was there. You wouldn't have to look for other ways.

"I don't want to hurt you," I began. "I just don't want you to think you have to do anything for me to be your friend. I'll be your friend anyway." Our eyes met. "I will." She finally believed me. "If I ever decide I want to make out with you—and I might—I don't want so much planning to go into it. I want it to be a great surprise for both of us."

Jessie smiled and told me that I was different.

To this day I have no idea whether she meant that as a compliment or not. I just couldn't orchestrate what was supposed to be one of the most wonderfully spontaneous moments of my life. When curious friends asked how the night had gone, I gave them dirty looks and told them to mind their own business. I'm not sure what conclusion they came to, because after that, Jessie's body became off-limits. She wore less makeup and spent less time trying to win over the boys. The last I heard about her was that she got a scholarship to a fancy boarding school in Rhode Island.

The truth about that night was simple. We played poker until three-thirty in the morning. We laughed a lot, and shared some Pepsi and a Snickers candy bar. When it came time to sleep, Jessie and I lay down together and held each other. The only things we took off were our sneakers. Maybe, just maybe, she could have been my fantasy princess. Mrs. McNeil's stories had been about magic, and it stood to reason that such magic could take many forms. I liked that, but this happily-ever-after stuff—well, that had to wait.

# A Farewell to Joey

It would have been a perfect summer day if the news about Joey hadn't come. Feeling sunny and lazy, I had only one thing on my mind—the Yankees game I would be listening to later on in the evening, provided that things remained peaceful enough. I often stole up to the roof where no one could find me. David joined me and worked on his drafting. If I was able to keep my parents at bay, it was a good day.

I had just come home from a guitar lesson at school. Because of the easy summer schedule, the only rule of this class was to show up at 8:00 A.M. and be willing to practice. Bruce Springsteen was quite impressive to me—so I reasoned I'd better learn to handle a guitar. The dancing and jumping around—the rhythm that David said I didn't have—would come later. I had sat next to a chunky kid named Homer who wanted to be just like B. B. King. He took a black magic marker and wrote *Lucille* across the soundbox of his guitar. I smiled at him every time he mastered a chord or was able to keep up with Mr. Jackson's instructions. Everybody wanted to be somebody—that was for sure.

I answered the phone on the third ring and Allison's frantic voice frightened me. I asked her to calm down because I couldn't understand her. I just knew that something was terribly wrong. That was when she told me that Joey's mother had gone into his room to wake him, and found him dead. She had no details and she kept repeating, "I can't take this."

I told her we would talk later. Then I flung my guitar in the closet and headed for the roof. No one would find me there, and it would give me some time to think about this. I couldn't stop shaking, so I took my Walkman from my pocket and blasted it. Maybe all that noise would distract me enough to make my heart calm down.

I had just seen Joey two nights before at a Central Park baseball game. He and David and I and several of our friends were playing against a team from the Bronx, with a twenty-dollar bet riding on the outcome. Sandy, Denise, and some other girls sat in the bleachers and cheered encouragement. They laughed too, as we made masterful attempts to be agile and professional and failed horribly at it. For some reason, you always play best when no one is watching. David dropped a backhanded catch in the outfield and proclaimed himself Mickey Mantle. Joey hit four foul balls in a row and blamed it on the wind. His brother Klein kept yelling to him to choke up on the bat. Joey turned to him, shook his rear end from side to side, and told his brother to stick to fashion design and leave the sports to him. Klein made a face and joined the girls in the bleachers to sulk. I had to laugh at his designer wristbands. That's why we called him Klein. His real name was Mitchell, but that didn't suit someone who was determined to surpass everyone else in the world of fashion. He was always drawing, always experimenting with different outfits and haircuts. He was temperamental, sometimes a bit touchy. I often found myself wanting to slap him on the head and tell him to stop taking himself so seriously. He enjoyed a deep sense of angst, got into being misunderstood and distant. Joey loved him, so we tolerated him. He always seemed to need protecting—a role that Joey took very seriously. When other kids picked on Klein, Joey warned them that they would have to fight him first. People liked Joey so much that it saved Klein's butt on more than one occasion. It was hard to believe sometimes that Klein was two years older than Joey.

As the game progressed, we laughed and made ridiculous errors as we screamed and cursed and threatened one another with all kinds of bodily harm. We won the game in the bottom of the ninth inning by one run. Joey let a line drive go, and it nearly made a soprano out of the shortstop, who stood looking as though he didn't realize he had the ball in his hand and that he could have tagged Billy out at home plate. We screamed and carried on—gave one another high fives, let the girls give us congratulatory kisses— and acted as though we had just won the World Series. We spent the twenty dollars on hot dogs and sodas within an hour. Everything was *so* okay!

And then this . . .

Joey and I had met in a class meant for physics and chemistry enthusiasts. We were labeled "eccentrics of the arts," and the other kids took pleasure in turning up their noses at us. To survive, we had to get to know each other. I realized soon that I liked him a great deal. There was more to Joey than his availability for a good prank. He idolized James Dean and could recite the entire *Rebel Without a Cause* script without hesitating. He had a photographic memory and was the greatest mimic. I never saw a person charm his way out of a missed homework assignment the way Joey could. He was silly and witty, always looking to play a prank on someone. Madly in love with Allison—as she was with him—he had the rest of their lives mapped out, although she was only twelve and he thirteen. She was going to stay home and paint masterpieces and fight for all of her needy causes, and he was going to knock them dead on the stage with his powerful performances. As he always said, he was going to give them his all—they were going to step inside his heart and soul. But on the day he died, I learned that there was a secret room within Joey that no one was allowed to step inside.

I went back to school hoping that Mr. Jackson would be there. I needed to talk to someone— about what, I didn't know. I just hoped he was there. I made up some excuse about forgetting my sheet music, and he told me to come in and look for it. He came and stood next to me and waited for me to look at him.

"I understand Joey was a good friend of yours," he said softly.

I nodded. "I just heard about it—but I don't know what happened." I sat up on the desk and tried to work a stubborn knot out of the lace of my sneaker. I had to do something—it felt as though my insides were going to come apart. The simplest solution never occurred to me. All I needed to do was tell Mr. Jackson that I was afraid. He squatted down, and with his large and clumsy fingers—fingers that I couldn't figure out how he handled a guitar with—removed the knot and continued talking, almost as if to ease the knot from my throat. He told me that Joey had overdosed on cocaine and choked while vomiting in his sleep. My mouth opened in disbelief. I let him hug me. He held me for a few minutes and let me cry, every so often telling me that it was all right.

"This isn't fair. We just played baseball the other day. If I'd known he was going to be dead in a few days, I would have said something important."

Mr. Jackson nodded and said, "It's not fair. We've got right now to work with and yesterday to reflect on. Tomorrow's a big maybe."

"Mr. Jackson, if I'd known, maybe I would have done something different. You always figure that things will be okay."

There were tears in his eyes when I looked up at him. "Never figure," he said softly. "Never figure."

I went with my friends to the funeral and resigned myself to expect the worst, to feel horrible—but I steeled myself to survive it. A quick glimpse of Klein reminded me to search for courage. His dark, straight hair was pushed back with no part and slicked down with grease, just like a gangster's. His black double-breasted suit was at least two sizes too big, and his dark glasses with side reflectors said that he didn't want anyone to know how much he cried. Everyone knew anyway. David found out that when the police and ambulance came to pick Joey up, Klein tried to beat them up as they placed his brother in a body bag. They tried to control him, but he threw himself on the ground and screamed so loud that the tenants even six floors above him shuddered. Hearing the story, all I could think about was how glad I was not to have been there.

I walked up to the coffin with David, and he immediately began to cry. Suddenly he screamed, "Why did you do this?" Billy and I pulled him into one of the lounges and sat quietly with him.

I was glad to be out of there. I wanted Joey to sit up, and with a corny Transylvanian accent say, "Fooled you!" It was just like him to go to such extremes for a joke, but this was no joke. He was so blue. That's what dead was. That's what scared the hell out of David.

I excused myself from everyone and stood outside for a few minutes. I took deep breaths and struggled to understand what I was feeling, because I was suddenly very angry at Joey. He had escaped the worst part of growing up in a bad neighborhood. People had respected him and regarded him as a genius. He had planned to go to college. The part of him that had survived in the world of the streets had never cowered from discomfort or questioned awful circumstances at home enough to let them tear him apart. It was a vicious circle, no matter what. It was obvious that Joey had succumbed to the same madness that he'd wanted to get away from. It was about pain relief. Joey often talked about his parents' violent fights, which frequently turned against him and Klein. Joey always appointed himself the sacrificial lamb and acted obnoxious, figuring that if they picked on him, they would leave each other and Klein alone. Ironically, here they stood—his father holding a strong arm around his mother as she cried.

I couldn't help thinking about myself and the many times when I'd wondered whether the struggle was all worth it. Just the night before, a siege with my parents had left me black and blue. It was because my father had decided that I was hanging out with hoodlums. He'd said that Joey had died because he was up to no good. He'd said that it served him right. That was the most hypocritical statement I had ever heard, so rather than respond, I just glared at him and bit my tongue not to say what I really thought. Later that evening, as David and I struggled to close up the gashes on my leg in the bathroom at Port Authority, he begged me to stay away from that snake. "Please, Tone. Don't let him near you anymore. I need you here. Everyone around us is dying."

Perhaps that was why I always waited before doing something like that. There was always the hope that maybe I had a chance—I held for dear life onto my "someday."

When I walked back into the funeral parlor and saw how devastated and upset people looked, I promised myself to do what I could to hang in, but Klein and Allison had begun to sing Springsteen songs. That was too bizarre for me, so I got up to leave the room again. Klein came after me and said, "You should have stayed to sing with us. This is my brother's last party, and you were his buddy. Oh, by the way, I need a favor. Really it's for Joey—you remember the variety show, right?"

"Dammit, Klein, come up for air."

"I just don't want to forget to tell you, that's all. Joey was crazy about the way you sang 'Forever' at the variety show, so all us guys decided that maybe you should sing it for the funeral tomorrow."

"I don't know, Klein," I said. "I'm not much in the mood to sing."

We were distracted by the bloodcurdling screams of a girl being led from the parlor by some older kids. I looked closer and shook my head. These were older kids who had hardly ever said hello to Joey, and that girl had once slapped Joey's face because he threw a kiss at her. This was incredible. Wall-to-wall people sharing the senselessness of this loss. Why couldn't just one of these people have let Joey know that they'd help him through one more day? Klein yelled out my name, and I turned again and looked at him.

"What do you say, will you sing it?"

I shrugged. It wasn't supposed to be this way. I figured that twenty years down the road we'd be sitting around talking over old times and I'd be thanking Joey for encouraging me to ask Denise to a party. Amen, Mr. Jackson. Never figure! I turned to Klein. "Okay, Klein, I'll sing it."

Klein reached over to hug me and began to cry. "I wish that he hadn't always thought he could beat the odds. He didn't understand that he didn't have to. Every time he got high or got away with something, he figured that he got over. Every time he got over, it made him sure that he was alive. It made him feel like he got away from the pain. My brother didn't understand that you never do get away from pain, but that pain can bring out the best part of you." He paused. "*I know.*"

For the first time I felt sorry for Klein. Joey had gotten away, and his pain was over. Klein was left to hold the bag with their parents and with all of the unanswered speculation about their lives. He would always wonder what he could have done to change things.

I thought about that all that day and the next morning, when I met David at his house for the funeral. Again he had a white shirt and a tie ready for me. His tie was already on, choking him. We got to the funeral home just as Joey's casket was being hoisted into the limousine. I couldn't imagine him being in there. The stifling heat was making me nauseous. I turned to David, who had a look of anger and contempt on his face, and asked him if he was all right.

"I'm just fine! He wanted to die? Good for him! Not me! I'm going to be here forever!" He loosened his tie and stormed inside the chapel ahead of me.

I took my place at the front, waited for the cue from the priest, and began.

"*Forever in my heart,*" I sang, straining to reach every note. "*And even when I'm gone, you'll be here with me . . . forever in my life.*"

Tears streamed down my face unashamedly as I acknowledged to myself that Joey would be forever in my life although I would never see him again. Death was final—there was no way to get it to change its mind. We were never going to see Joey again. That's what David was so sore about.

*"Forever!"* I repeated, as I hit that powerful last note, while Klein, David, and some of our classmates took their places as pallbearers. The ties, jackets, and ninety-degree heat made me long for dirty T-shirts and a baseball game for twenty dollars, a few hot dogs, and some laughs. I had never taken the time to understand how wonderful that was. I did understand, though, that forever was a long time.

# Turning Away

It took a few months and many sleepless and tearful nights before I could resign myself to the fact that Joey was gone and there was nothing that I could do about it. As David and I sped back and forth on the trains at night, I kept dreaming over and over that I was stopping Joey from choking. David often had to shake me awake and tell me that I was calling too much attention to myself. I told him what was happening in the dreams, and he shook his head.

"Leave it alone, Tone. He's dead—just face it. We've got enough crap going on." Then he'd suggest nonchalantly that I go back to sleep because he wasn't too tired anyway.

He was right. I did have more crap going on than I could deal with. Things were getting progressively worse at home, and it had become increasingly difficult to cope. I wasn't smart enough to be as concerned as David was about it. My denial was hurting me as much as the incidents themselves, which were becoming more frequent. It was getting harder and harder to cover up their aftereffects. When I wasn't wincing from pain, I was struggling to shake off my horrible feelings about myself. I told myself that these hardships were temporary, that soon I would be out and away from this nightmare. If I thought about it for more than a few seconds, though, I doubted it.

Riding trains at night was a last-ditch attempt to get a good night's sleep—and that wasn't working anymore. Joey's death was my first lesson in finality. I couldn't get it through my head that no matter how much I wanted to turn the clock back, I would never see Joey again. I was soon to learn, however, that it is harder yet to let go of someone who is alive.

Joey's death sent Allison on a steady downhill path. All of the goals that she'd set for herself were gone. She abandoned her ambitions to be a painter or to work with troubled kids by teaching them about colors and creativity. She no longer wanted to tell people that they were worth something. She didn't want to rescue innocent mice—she didn't care who wore fur coats anymore. She cut so many classes that she was kicked out of the progressive program. No amount of covering for her and handing in assignments for her could have prevented it. Eventually she stopped going to school. She hijacked any written correspondence about her truancy from the mailbox, and when the attendance officer came to the door, she ignored the knocking. It was easy for her to get away with this because her parents paid such little attention to her and her life. They would leave her messages on the answering machine, telling her they were going away for the weekend. Denise visited and found Allison—at four in the afternoon—still in her pajamas and snorting cocaine. She had enough money to pay for it because her parents never even questioned what she needed the money for. I shook my head when I heard this. Allison had been the type of person who wouldn't take aspirin because she considered it a chemical.

David said to let her be. He claimed that she was smart enough to know that all of these things were harmful. If she was doing them, he reasoned, it was because she wanted to. He felt that we had no business trying to find out why. People were entitled to their own misery. I thought back to the summer seminar that many of us had attended in upstate New York the year before. I had become frustrated at the amount of work I couldn't complete. I was ready to throw in the towel when Allison came into the room and smiled at me. "You think you've got it bad," she giggled. "At least you don't have to draw the bottoms of tables and chairs." I looked at her sketchpad and noticed at least eight attempts. "We have all night," she said cheerfully. "You'll learn that and I'll get this." We did, too—after having gone through three batches of popcorn and two six-packs of Pepsi. Angie sat across from us, trying to master the different parts of the brain. We didn't have the heart to tell her that the cup after cup of decaffeinated coffee that she drank was not what was keeping her awake. The power of suggestion was stronger than any of us had known. We got to bed at seven in the morning, but I was happy.

"I'll go see her," I told Denise. "We'll get her back."

I took my seat on the subway and tried to look away from the woman across from me, who was tripping. No, I thought. No matter how much Allison experimented with drugs, she could never get that bad. She was special, and that gave her an exclusive insurance policy. As the train screeched to a sudden halt, I remembered being five years old and sitting in a waiting room outside a speech therapist's office. Speaking in a tone loud enough for me to hear, the therapist had urged my teacher and the principal to place me in a "special program." Translation: dummy class. I would never speak correctly, she stated with haughty certainty. My stuttering and lisp would *always* be there. My parents were notified, and I was beaten for embarrassing them. They made it clear from that time that they would not take well to complaints and confrontations. That began my pattern of keeping a low profile and making every attempt to divert attention from myself. My father had told me that if I couldn't talk right, I shouldn't talk at all. Feeling helpless, defeated, and quite worthless, I succumbed to my own solution: I stopped talking completely.

One afternoon a few weeks after I had stopped

talking, an accident in the schoolyard gave me a bloody nose. I stood fast against a wall as blood saturated the front of my shirt. Kids stood around, pointing and saying that I was gross, but I didn't budge. Seeing this, the principal picked me up and carried me into his office, where he stopped the bleeding, cleaned me up, and sat me on his lap and rocked me for a long time. When the secretary came in to ask him something, he said that he was busy and didn't want to be interrupted. For several moments he said nothing, and then he turned me around to face him.

"If you don't ever want to talk again, that's up to you. But it doesn't mean that if something hurts or if you're in trouble, you don't deserve for someone to help you." I looked hard at his face to ask whether he'd meant it. "You're special—so special," he said as he held me. "We're all special."

Within six months my speech improved, and I was able to skip kindergarten and go into the first grade because my reading and writing skills were advanced enough. From time to time I would see the principal in the schoolyard and wave to him. He'd smile that same smile I remembered—the one he had when he told me I was special. I looked forward to seeing him. He knew my name and he was always ready for a hug. Sometimes he visited the classes and read stories to the children. Once he was leaving school with a handful of balloons and a big basket of fruit. He called me over and told me to pick something out from the basket, and handed me a blue metallic balloon. A few months later, he suddenly wasn't there. A woman with a mean stare took over his office. The YES I CAN and READING IS MAGIC posters came down. Five years later, while eavesdropping upon a conversation between two teachers, I heard he had died. He'd lost his job when his HIV-positive status was found out. One of the first to get caught by the "gay plague," he had gotten almost no support from family or coworkers. Those who weren't afraid of him were disappointed in him. Everything wonderful in him was overlooked and pushed aside. He died in a hospice, with a priest reading prayers to him. The teachers who were expressing their sympathy couldn't see their way clear to being sorry that they had never paid a visit or sent a card. They just "felt bad" because he had gotten mixed up in "the wrong life-style." One of them said it was a waste because he was so good-looking. Tears filled my eyes as I pretended not to hear them. *He* was special, and probably no one had told him so. I wasn't sure whether I cried for him or because no one said anything truly kind. I wondered if this was just a small introduction to the world I was to grow up in—a world of cold and judgmental indifference that left no room for anything special. I was suddenly afraid of what kind of man I would grow up to be.

I looked across the subway car at the stoned-out woman again. Our eyes met and I smiled.

Surprisingly, she smiled back. Maybe no one had told her that she was special. That's what love was—letting people know that you would hold them because they were special. I was determined to remind Allison.

When she opened the door, Allison made it obvious that she was less than thrilled to see me. I tried to hug her, but she stepped away. When I asked if it was okay for me to come in, she said, "Okay, I guess, if you want to." I walked into the room after her, and asked her if she was still the teddy bear's number-one fan. She always decorated her books, her locker, and her clothes with different types of teddy bears, because she thought they were cute and cuddly and always available for a hug. David reminded her every once in a while that real bears killed. She shook her head at my question, and held up Jim Morrison's biography.

I smiled, hoping that she would too. "Isn't he the guy who wanted to light everyone's fire?"

The old Alli would have chuckled with me. Not this one. She glared like a dragon. She said that this life we led held nothing good, and if I was smart, I'd truly understand that fact.

"That's your fact, not mine," I said, trying to convince myself as much as to persuade her. This sudden and abrupt cynicism gave me a horrible feeling. Then, to change the subject, I smiled again and asked, "Do you still mispronounce words?"

She shrugged. "Who knows? Who cares?"

"Don't you care about anything anymore, Alli?" She shook her head impatiently and stared at the TV as I badgered her. "What's happened to you, Allison? You were always so caring."

"Caring is nothing but a frustration. I choose to be practical."

"But your sense of caring was always the best part of you. Hey! You're the one who conned me into going out to build a snowman during a blizzard because you said that no one was too old to do that."

"The snowman melted away, didn't it, Tony? It didn't come back again someday like the song promised."

"So what! Something else came along! Spring-time, baseball games—all of those things you always loved." She raised her eyes intolerantly as I went on, struggling to move her. I was becoming frightened at her attitude. I didn't even want to imagine that there was no "someday" waiting to happen for me.

"Come on, Alli. Where's the friend who told me that things were going to be great for me—who encouraged me to go on, no matter what?"

"She's a ghost of your past. Leave it that way." We sat in painful silence for five minutes and then she asked, "Why did you come here?"

"I came to tell you that you were special," I said.

"That doesn't move me one way or another."

Like it or not, I had to let go. I couldn't accompany her on that path to hell without leaving a part of myself there, and I wasn't willing to do that. I thought about myself and my circle of friends. People looked at us with admiration and confidence. They never understood the price we paid as we struggled between that world of childhood and adulthood. People were rarely around to help us get unstuck whenever we felt as though we were trapped between the two worlds. Our intelligence was never a help when it came time to wrestle with our hearts.

From time to time I still hear about Allison through someone else. She sleeps until midafternoon, and the high point of her life is watching "The David Letterman Show." I received a note from her some months ago:

> *In writing this letter I feel as though I am connecting to a life that I once lived but no longer consider a part of me. . . . At once I am confused as to why I am writing . . . the reason is a curious nostalgia. . . . Most of the faces, names, lives of those people I knew when I knew you have melted into an indistinguishable pool of memory. . . . But you—you haunt me. . . . Some odd thing has happened until I succumbed to the urge to contact you. . . . The real criminal is the question why—the one that never fails to accompany a thought of you. . . . My life is insane—mundane . . . not quite a life at all . . . it more resembles an existence . . . or an imitation. The air is dull and I am breathing as if I were drowning. . . . Who are you, now?*

I called to tell her that I was still the same person who helped her to rescue the mice. I struggled to make her realize that she would be all right if she just made a conscious effort to try. I knew at that point that she wasn't hearing me, but I thought of the feelings I had at Joey's funeral, where I'd wished that someone could have made Joey push for one more day. She couldn't talk because she was getting ready to watch the tape of last night's David Letterman. I told her I loved her and she said, "Yeah, okay, we'll talk."

I doubt we ever will. Allison was gone—just a casualty of circumstances she chose to suffer through by herself. My grief said she was gone—the look in her eye on the day of Joey's funeral did, too. David was wrong when he said that "nobody died for nobody."

A cold and lonely feeling came over me as I hung up the phone. No one had ever told me that you couldn't force someone to be special.

# Bomber Jackets and Broken Hearts

Whoever says that the growing-up years are the best of your life must have spent a childhood with a tutor who made the outside world seem like something it wasn't. Almost as a continuation of happily-ever-after stories, it's amazing how often the world is depicted as a wonderfully curious place, full of splendor and beauty. Sometimes, maybe—and I was always open to that. Other times the world is just dark and bleak and plain ugly. People are often ugly too, and you don't need to look long to see that. Many people don't hide their ugliness, but the ones who do are much more dangerous because their victims are unaware, open, and defenseless. Kids can be cruel and ruthless. There is nothing as devastating as peer pressure, nothing that can crush your self-esteem as much as not being seen as you want to be seen. Once a kid gets to the point where he understands what an outer image is, he or she becomes a slave to it and it takes over his or her inner image as well.

Everything matters: clothes, hairstyles, how well you can dance—or how smooth your reasoning is for not doing so if you can't. Intelligence, athletic skill, and ability to be respected by an older crowd are definite advantages. It is well worth it to get into a fistfight to achieve such status. Competition is fierce for everything. Everyone struggles to come across as if they make no effort at all, and girls aren't the only ones consumed with their appearance. Guys are just as vain—or worse. I know. I stood in front of a mirror every morning and combed my hair just so. I once overheard one of the girls talking about how naturally my hair waved at the top. Naturally, my butt! That wave was the product of long and arduous training—all in an effort to receive such a compliment and be able to act indifferent to it. The competition became overwhelming, especially when I was feeling like I had no desire to be suave and indifferent. Sometimes I just wanted to be a little kid and color pictures or listen to "The Muppets' Greatest Hits" as opposed to whatever played on the Top 40. I would've been crucified for admitting it too.

There was a girl in my English class named Clara, whose parents were strict and didn't allow her to dress in anything fashionable. She came to school in dumpy-looking dresses and black tie shoes of the kind that nuns wore. Kids constantly ragged her when she walked out into the schoolyard. They'd call out, "Hey, gorgeous!" and throw her kisses. They'd make sarcastic remarks about her clothes. Because of this, she never looked at anyone and always walked with her head down. She got hysterical one day when Artie threw her a kiss and mouthed "I love you"—she screamed and cried and banged her head into her locker. It took two teachers to drag her down to the nurse's office, and we could still hear the piercing screams as they closed the door. That frightened me—and it frightened me even more when Clara stopped coming to school and Denise found out that she had had to be put in the hospital. I felt ashamed that I'd never gotten to know her, but I didn't because she annoyed me when she wouldn't defend herself. When our homeroom teacher suggested making a card for her, I offered to draw it, despite the ribbing from guys who said that she was my woman. I made a unicorn and a rainbow and a bouquet of flowers. Even though I couldn't say the words, I wanted to relay the message to Clara that I cared. I never wanted to get to the point where my screams wouldn't be able to stay inside of me.

Shortly after Clara disappeared, David got into a mood where he was never satisfied with the way he looked. He hated his clothes, his hair, and his face. He thought that he was too short. He was angry at looking too ethnic.

"Face it, Tone," he'd say disgustedly. "I'm so typical. I've got a black father and a Puerto Rican mother—so does half of New York City."

"It doesn't matter, David," I said. "You're unique. You have good features."

He wasn't convinced. In fact, he laughed at me. "Good features? Unique? You're out of your mind! That's easy for you to say—you're so damn all-American with that light hair and those blue eyes. *You're* the one with the right features. You'll never sweat anything."

That cliche about the grass always looking greener on the other side of the fence has some truth to it because I, on the other hand, felt that I was ordinary—that I lacked coolness. And beyond that, I had never told even David how often those people that my parents forced me to be with always said something about wanting to be with someone as pretty as me. Some said I was cute enough to be a girl. David had no idea how many times I was tempted to take a knife or a razor blade and slash my face—maybe, I thought, it would have made me less appealing and I would not have despised looking in the mirror as much as I did. It was all a matter of perception and a very fragile sense of self. Both of ours were way off. It got scary, though, when David's distorted perception of himself nearly drove him over the edge.

It all began when bomber jackets became a very "in" thing at school. Most of the guys were getting them, and David wanted one desperately. His mother told him to forget it, that she refused to spend a hundred and fifty dollars when he already had a perfectly good coat. I had gotten my hands on a shabby secondhand jacket because someone in the building gave it to my father. He told me to take it for myself and acted as though he had given me something out of this world. I didn't like it, I just wore it because it kept the cold away. It was too big on me, and I would have preferred a baseball jacket. People at school began to compliment me on it, and of course I pretended to be pleased. That was when David's obsession with getting a bomber jacket escalated. He slipped me a note during class and told me to cut gym and meet him at our usual hiding spot in the auditorium.

"This better be real interesting," I said in a most annoyed fashion. I was missing field hockey.

He smiled. "Relax, would you? I have an idea. How would you like to be able to afford the best clothes in New York?"

"Is Daddy Warbucks going to adopt us?"

He reached over and slapped my head. "This is serious. Stay with me here." I continued to make faces as he spoke. "Tone, there are a bunch of rich old men hanging around in Times Square. I hear they pay an awful lot for some company."

I laughed out loud. "Do you know what the hell you're *saying*? Do you know what they'll want?"

David scoffed. "We can work around that. We'll make them pay up front."

" 'We' nothing!" I shouted, as I realized that

David was taking this hustling stuff seriously. "How the hell do you know what kind of a creep you'll hook up with?"

He was visibly angry at me, and the feeling had begun to be mutual. "Forget it!" he shouted back. "I didn't think you'd be scared to go after something you want!"

It was my turn to become enraged at his attempt to belittle me. I picked up my books and headed for the door. Then I turned back to look at him, tempted to punch him, and said, "I'm not scared of a damn thing—get that straight!" He crossed his arms across his chest and positioned his feet on the seat in front of him as I continued. "And as far as going after something I want—I want to do just what I'm doing and keep as much crap out of my life as I can. Right now I'm going back to gym. If I can make up a good enough story about being late, I might get myself into the field hockey game. That's what *I* want!" David turned his face as I stormed out.

I ran all the way to the gym, where I got into two fights during the field hockey game. Once was because Tim shoved me aside to get at the puck and the other time was because someone on the other team called me a "pretty boy." I punched him so hard that he bit his lower lip. He was nearly double my weight, and he pushed me into the wall and almost choked me. Mr. Graham, the teacher, told me to take a shower and to report to his office. I needed a shower, too. I felt dirty, disgusted, and very angry. Fortunately, the shower room was empty and no one could see the latest set of bruises my parents had inflicted on me. For fifteen minutes I rubbed my skin raw and ran water as hot as I could stand it all over myself. My thoughts were exhausting, and though I tried to push them away, they flooded back. I had gotten to the point where I gauged things by saying, "At least I'm alive." There was no question that I wanted to be. There were a few momentary lapses, however—like right then, when it would have been more than all right with me if I died. I felt a darkness descending and surrounding me, and nothing would make it leave me alone.

When I sat down in the chair across from Mr. Graham, he smiled at me. "Bad day, Tony?" Mr. Graham always called everyone by his first name. This effort at personalization made a lump form in my throat, and I shrugged. I was torn between wanting to respond to his overture and remaining in my typical guarded mode. He turned on the radio, and the song "Don't Let the Sun Go Down on Me" was playing. How appropriate! Lately it always felt like it was getting harder and harder to see daylight.

"I'm sorry about the game, Mr. Graham. I won't fight next week."

Mr. Graham waited until our eyes met, and then he winked at me. "I asked you to stop and talk because I wanted to know if there was anything you needed to talk about."

Sure, I thought, if he had about three days

and a room in his basement to hide me in. It was nice that he asked, but the truth was that I couldn't talk to anyone, so I just shook my head and said no thank you.

He continued to fish. "You looked pretty angry at something." I could just see me telling this man that there were bruises all over my arms and legs and that I hadn't had any good sleep in two days. It would just bring more chaos; it would only buy me more problems, and at this point I had too many. At least I used to think David had good sense and that he would help me to feel less alone. "I'm just angry at myself, Mr. Graham. I promise to act better next time."

I hoped he would let me off the hook and give me a pass back to class, but he didn't. I was afraid I would cry—terrified that I wouldn't be able to keep things to myself.

"Tony," he said kindly, "something that had nothing to do with field hockey was eating at you today. If you don't want to say what, that's fine, but let's make a deal, all right?" I nodded, knowing that it was the only way I was going to get out of there. "If anything gets so bad within the next couple of days—or ever—you come and see me. I'd hate to hear that you did something stupid because you felt that there was no one you could talk to."

"Thanks, Mr. Graham, I will," I said nervously, as he wrote out a late pass. I wished I could take him up on that—wished I could tell him the truth—wished I could cry—wished I could be someone else. None of that was possible, so I had to settle for being myself and praying that things would stay on an even keel.

I left school that day without talking to David. We weren't going to agree—that was obvious—and I didn't want to talk anymore about Times Square. This was not the first time I had heard about kids going there to sell themselves for clothes or spending money. One kid in our history class bought his family's groceries that way. I couldn't, though—I didn't want even one more person putting his slimy hands on me, and I was deeply angry at David for even suggesting it.

It was close to midnight when he showed up at my apartment looking for me, visibly shaken. "Tone, you want to go ride the trains?"

I grabbed my jacket and hurried out the door with him. At one point as we stood on the platform waiting for the train, he approached the edge too closely and I grabbed his arm. A funny feeling came over me—he knew better than that. I gave him a stern look, as if to say, *Don't even try it.* We took our seats at the back of the car, and David turned to me with tears in his eyes.

I put my arm around his shoulder. "You went to Times Square, right?"

He leaned against me and cried for a long time. "I never thought it would be like this," he repeated over and over. "I never thought it would." I repeated almost the same words in my own head: I *knew* that it would.

David cried for what seemed like hours. I don't

know when it happened that I joined him. I couldn't tell him that it would be all right, though I wanted to so badly. I knew, though, that it never would be again. It was as if you had been dusted with a cloud of smoke that neither clothes nor good feelings could cover up. Once someone invades that part of you that is sacred and private, nothing much feels right again. I was scared, too, because I didn't want to lose David. It seemed as though the little bit of a world that I had with him was caving in. His need had become such an obsession with him that I wasn't sure whether it would be possible to get him to defuse it, and I was afraid that it was going to take over every part of him and get him into trouble. It all had to do with want—with those things that were lacking and their almost lethal effect. When well-meaning teachers like Mr. Graham offered their ear, they were unaware of how complex such a situation was. A heart-to-heart and a pat on the back wouldn't cut it. It was going to take much more than a good talk to fix all that was wrong here. David dug his nails into my arm and looked up at me.

"Do you know what I did, Tone?"

I sure did. I knew what he was going to do before he did it. That's what made me so angry. I wanted to scold him and say, "I told you so," and ask whether a jacket was worth it. The mournful look on his face changed my mind. He was never going to forget this—and that was punishment enough.

I shook my head. "I don't need to know—it's over."

"I wanted that jacket so bad. I needed a solution—after all, it's not like I could run to Mommy and Daddy and ask them for it." The bitterness of that statement hit home. I sure could relate to not being able to ask for anything. I didn't even think along those lines.

David whimpered. "Everyone said it would be so easy. I wanted easy—and I wanted that jacket. I still want it, Tone. Why is that so wrong?"

It wasn't wrong, and at the same time it changed nothing. I ripped the jacket off my back as if there were something contagious on it, and ordered him to take off his sweatshirt. "Come on, trade with me."

"No, I'm not taking yours."

"Trade with me or I'll pull that sweatshirt off your back." He didn't budge. "I hate this damn thing. It's only a *thing*, David—an inanimate *thing*! Just take it! It's making you miserable, and I don't care one way or another about it. *Things* are not that important." I was crying again. "*You're* important, David. That's all."

We exchanged clothing—tears falling down his face as he took the jacket from me. Gently he folded it, positioned it underneath his head, and fell asleep.

Confusion overcame me. I could feel the subway vibrate. I heard the screeching of the wheels on the tracks, and each time the light flickered on and off, I held my breath. From the moment when we draw our first breath, we begin to want. First it's a bottle, or maybe a diaper-changing, a hug, or a toy. Before we know it, our tastes develop, along with our self-perception, and we get into trouble. What could the solution be? Here we were, eleven years old, and already we were feeling the anger and guilt of wanting. Would it get better when we got older? Would we care as much? David had literally sold his body for a want—for a piece of leather, a couple of scraps of material that he thought were going to make him feel better about himself. I thought of why kids got into drugs, gangs, and premature sex. They wanted possessions, position, and love. I wanted those things too, but I was determined to wait—then I would be sure that nothing would slap me in the face. I was going to be smart and secure in knowing that I had made all of the right moves. I promised myself that once I did that, I would never turn back.

Ironically, David used the twenty dollars from that pickup to buy a handful of subway tokens and several packs of gum—tools to help him escape and forget about what was really important. They would help him soften what was. David cried as he told me that the guy had ordered him to do things he couldn't ever imagine people doing. I not only *could* imagine those things, I could close my eyes and feel them. I remembered every touch, every smell, and how much my body would cringe when the terror of these things would set in. I didn't have the heart or the courage to tell him that chewing gum only works for a while, and then you begin to despise the taste of spearmint. He would find out soon enough that the times when he felt at peace ever again would be few and far between.

David and I never talked about that incident again. When other kids mentioned going to Times Square, a strange look crossed his face, as if someone had just punched him in the stomach. He'd look away and take a deep breath, and if our eyes met, I'd smile at him and shake my head as if to say, *Leave it alone.*

He wore that beat-up old bomber jacket to school every day, and acted cocky and self-assured whenever someone complimented him on it. I noticed how sometimes he would stand back and admire himself in a store window—a strange and satisfied smile crossing his lips. When he took it off, he always hung it up carefully in his locker.

David and I continued to ride trains and talk about what we wanted. Someday we would be able to open a wallet and pay for something just because we wanted it. We longed for the day when it wouldn't feel as though that list of wants was so long. We silently prayed to know, finally, that wanting was all right. In our world, that was just too much to ask sometimes, but we tried. We did what we could, and we bit the bullet when we had to. We were no heroes, nor were we practiced or experienced at handling situations that got the better of us. We were friends, though, and we knew that if there was no one else, the other was there to cushion the avalanche of perplexing emotions. We went on because there was simply no reason not to yet. Somehow I knew that if there was a God, He'd know that we wanted—that our hearts broke because of it—that we were alive in spite of it.

# *True Blue*

When it comes down to it, we all hold fast to our own realities. Pop says that we *are* our truths. We can't hide or run away from them, so we might as well celebrate them. I think of the many notable people who took drastic stands to do this: Henry David Thoreau, Martin Luther King, and—depending upon what you believe—Jesus Christ.

Who we are is reflected in the clothes we wear, the music we listen to, the company we keep. These things say a great deal about what we like and how we want others to see us. The problem within this society—which is supposed to be the most sophisticated in the world—is that the less popular choices are met with fierce opposition. Many people are forced to conceal their reality and betray their truths. Others choose to live a lie rather than having to contend with discrimination. After all, we're taught to follow the rules.

I learned a little about all this when, in order to get community involvement credits, David, Allison, and I got involved with a special tutoring program after school. For two weeks we were assigned to the kindergarten. I don't remember when I had so much fun. The most captivating thing about the kids was their lack of inhibition—their very bold honesty. One little boy in particular, Joshua, really made me laugh. He had curly brown hair and squinty brown eyes. He refused to sit in his seat. Why? Because he wanted to try out all of the seats. His good friend was a black kid named Jarvis. They drank out of each other's drink boxes, held hands when they walked together to the bathroom. Conventionality be damned, they were having a terrific time. They colored purple trees and green men with yellow faces. They didn't explain why, either. That was when it hit me. All of the hang-ups of our society and all of the prejudices within our world are carefully taught.

The year I turned eleven, I went to the annual Gay and Lesbian Pride Parade along Fifth Avenue. I wanted to write a report about it for a school paper because the newspapers said that they expected a great turnout. The papers talked about the AIDS crisis and how this gathering would give gay people ample forum to address the crucial issues. I didn't know exactly what AIDS was, but I did know that every time I heard about it, there was some kind of gay connection. It was leered at in school bathrooms or whispered by adults that this disease was a homosexual thing. Translation: Let them deal with it.

One columnist, obviously opposed to the parade, said that it was a good excuse for a loud and rowdy bunch to cause trouble. He intimated that it was all they were about.

As far as I ever knew, people never admitted to being gay. When they did, they were ostracized, ridiculed, and discredited as people. How many times did I hear snickering just at the mention of the word? I figured you had to have rocks in your head to admit openly that you were gay. I wanted to know who would be so brazen about it. I needed to understand what the big deal was. What was the reason for separating? Weren't people just people? As I was to learn apparently not. One bigoted teacher of mine smiled after congratulating me for wanting to research such a story. "People might be people," he said, "but they're strange people." I asked why and he couldn't answer. I would see for myself—for personal reasons of my own.

It's not that I was so liberal or that I even knew a great deal about alternative life-styles. The world that I was subjected to was filled with, among other unpleasant things, homosexual occurrences. Sexual activity between two or more men, or between men and young boys, was quite common in my parents' sordid circle. The thing was that the very men who forced me to participate in sexual acts with them never talked about being gay. On the contrary, they spoke out adamantly against what they called "faggots." I knew a few who were gay-bashers and quite proud of it. My father declared that "fags" didn't deserve to live, and he bragged about the hard time he gave gay people every chance that he got. He called me a faggot because I read books and liked to draw, and threatened that if he ever caught me doing something with another guy, he would castrate me. Yet I was a witness—and a party—to many things he did that were far from heterosexual. I observed the pleasure he got from doing sexual things with other men and with me. For that reason I could not understand the difference between the violent life that I was being forced to live and a parade that demanded freedom of sexual choice.

A favorite teacher of mine had been fired for being daring enough to reveal his true self. He told another teacher that he was gay, and the next thing we knew, a permanent substitute teacher took his place. Word circulated around school that he'd been fired so that he wouldn't corrupt our minds with his ideas. Those ideas damaged me, too—ideas about poetry and reading and understanding literature for its own sake. He'd always reserve ten minutes at the end of each period to read to us. His voice was melodic as he piqued our curiosity by reading only the first chapters of classics like *The Count of Monte Cristo, Les Miserables,* and *A Tale of Two Cities.* I can still hear him as he began: "It was the best of times, it was the worst of times." He always saw to it that a few copies of each book were in his room, should anybody want to borrow one.

He put up a contest chart, and each semester the person who had handed in the most book reports got a bookstore gift certificate—a prize, I should add, that came out of his own pocket. He read *Jonathan Livingston Seagull* to us. If, in fact, that seagull could talk, I know he sounded like this teacher. He noticed I borrowed the class copy several times, even after I had written the report, so he pulled me aside one afternoon and handed me a brand-new copy for myself. I thanked him and he smiled and told me to keep those words close to me.

Oh yeah, he sure was an awful influence. So awful that late at night when I struggled to get my bearings after a siege with my father, I'd sit back and hear this man's voice in my head, words that were comforting me enough to get through the night. What he did when the school day was over never even occurred to me. It was the same as my principal from kindergarten. He also experienced heinous treatment as a result of being gay. Since they both made a pronounced difference in my life and made me feel human, I was determined to keep an open mind. Whatever this "gay" stuff was, it never interfered with their efforts to make me have a better day—on the contrary, sometimes they got me through a day. It was for the two of them that I went to the parade—to try to figure out what was so terrible about the way they lived—and why people seemed to think it was all right that so many were dying.

What was most obvious at this gathering was that people chose not to understand gay people. It made me angry to hear the taunts from on-lookers across the street and to see members of the clergy—supposedly representatives of God—making faces and inappropriate comments and passing judgment. But it didn't seem to discourage the marchers. I marveled as a few ostentatious demonstrators shouted back and encouraged others to cheer them on. It didn't take long before I silently cheered their unity. It seemed to me they were no different from any other group throughout history that had been oppressed. The energy and spirit were infectious. I wondered why I had not been this enthusiastic about anything in such a long time. I smiled when a very effeminate man proclaiming "gay power" fainted from exuberance—or maybe it was just the heat. Whatever it was, I admired him for being so real in front of so many. I had trouble going beyond telling people my name. It was clear that there was more to this than men who wanted to be campy and women who wanted to be butch. This was no freak show, as many of the spectators shouted. No one bothered me, even though they were screaming that gay people were child molesters. I suddenly became angry at the accusation. I listened as many of the marchers spoke. What they wanted was a chance not to hide. They wanted to be proud of who they were. This was about acceptance, about not wanting to live closeted in a makeshift existence that didn't offend anyone—except themselves. It was about no longer damning themselves and celebrating the fact that they weren't willing to live a lie anymore. I could relate to it. No one knew who I was, either, and at that point I couldn't think of a single person I could be a hundred percent honest with—not even David. Some of the shame cemented in my heart was so hidden even he couldn't know about it.

I thought of the many times when I heard one classmate refer to another as a faggot. To be so labeled was a fate worse than death. When one guy in our class took to wearing girls' clothes to school, the teasing was cruel and endless. On several occasions he was beaten up. David and I intervened once because a couple of guys had him pinned against the wall and one was threatening to castrate him. When he tried to thank us, we were less than gracious.

"You know, you could save yourself a lot of crap if you gave your sister her dress back," David said impatiently.

"This is just what I am," he said matter-of-factly.

From where I sit today, I wish I could have been so honest at that point in my own life.

The teachers began to take him less seriously, regardless of the fact that he kept his grades in the high nineties. The same lack of regard was extended to other minority classmates. The concept of marching to the beat of your own drummer doesn't mean very much. Why?

I stood watching and listening for close to two hours. People were being genuine, committed, and very loving to one another. They talked with emotion and passion about AIDS, and about people they loved who had suffered with it. They wanted to fight back against AIDS and get people to care. What could be so wrong with that? Didn't people fight to combat cancer and Alzheimer's disease? Why was AIDS any different, and why didn't the government do more to help? This was scaring me. I'm an American, and all I've ever heard is that I'm lucky to live in the greatest country in the world. I wasn't seeing much evidence of that. It rang out loud and clear that someone always had to be picked on. It's always been necessary for the oppressed to fight back. That reality was exhausting!

I completed the paper and got an A for detail. Some of my friends told me I was crazy for having gone there. After all, a few said, people could get the wrong idea. I asked them what made the idea wrong, and they thought I was kidding. They wanted to know whether I had discovered something strange about myself. Billy pulled me aside and assured me that I could confide in him. He wanted me to give it to him straight. Was I a faggot? I asked him what he would do if I was. He giggled and coughed and couldn't answer for a long time. I was really getting it. People will love you as long as you follow all of the rules. Don't rock the boat, and if your reality is too controversial, keep it to yourself. That stank!

I studied Billy's perplexed expression. Slowly his attitude toward me was changing, and I could see it happening. What had brought about that change? Judgment? Fixed morality? Maybe it was just a fear of something that he didn't know anything about. He continued to badger me, and I realized it was very important to him that I answer the question. I knew, too, that my response would determine the future status of our friendship.

"Come on, Tone, are you a faggot?"

I decided to be cagey. "What do you think?"

"I think you're not a sicko," he said.

"You're right about that." I patted his back and walked away, disheartened by the look of relief on his face. No, I wasn't a sicko. What I'd learned from the parade was that people didn't have to explain about themselves, they just had to be who they were.

I'm a little older now and understand better the principles of sexuality. I think Pop said it best: "Closing a bedroom door doesn't prove that you're a man or a woman. Being the best person that you can be and making love in a caring and mutual way does."

I think about that often, especially when memories of the nightmare return to threaten the peace I have tried to attain. I'm haunted by the flashback of Jake, relieving himself with my body the way that a drunken sailor uses a toilet, recklessly, vigorously, and savagely. The worst consequence of his actions is not the AIDS wreaking havoc in my body, but the indelibly damaging words that he spoke, and the cruelty from which he derived so much pleasure. I remember Jake and my father doubled over with laughter because I was too unsteady to stand up straight. These were the same men who called me a faggot and threatened to make me wear a dress because I cried. Jake said that I would never be a man. It was because of his violent assault on me that I won't.

Much blame and disapproval about life-styles and AIDS is directed at the gay community. I've come to realize that such judgments arrive by virtue of difference. I know that many people who are HIV-positive or who have died from AIDS were not infected in the same brutal way that I was. What has happened to me bears no relation to the morality of the homosexual community. My assailants weren't gay, they were vicious.

That parade taught me more than I expected to learn. The people there were real, and their demonstration proclaimed their truth. No one wanted to hurt or offend. Their intention was to bring about a special unity that would create awareness, pride, and admiration in others and in themselves. I wished that I could someday learn to admire myself.

Although there is a great deal in my life today

that allows me to feel good about myself, there are dark moments that intrude from time to time and don't allow me the right to know my own worth. Abraham Lincoln talked about how at the time of his death he would have at least one friend—the friend that lived deep inside of him. I learned about the friend inside of me by standing on the corner during a loud and unpopular parade.

# Scott, Dogface, and the Boys of Summer

If you were to ask me what was my favorite month, I'd have to say April. All of the leftover winter fades away, daylight stays later into the evening, and most of the hibernation ends. There isn't so much of a rush to get from one place to another to escape the cold. The world doesn't feel so lonely. There are more joggers, bike riders, and picnickers in Central Park. Relaxed and carefree, people sit reading under the trees. Mothers push baby carriages. Executives open up their ties and sling their jackets over their shoulders as they savor a good pushcart hot dog and a newspaper on a park bench. They'll even smile sometimes if you catch their eye.

Mornings are always the best for me in spring. I love the feeling of wearing only a short-sleeved shirt and walking to school as a coquettish breeze blows on my back. It's so much happier than feeling the hard, brisk wind against my bones. Shop owners stand outside their stores;

some sweep the sidewalk, and others wave to those passing as they exchange trivia about the ball game of the night before, ask about relatives, or comment about what a nice day it is. Even though they aren't talking to me, I enjoy it.

Across the street from my school was a special-ed facility that had an enrollment of three hundred or more students with problems ranging from Down's syndrome to cerebral palsy. It was easy for the students in my progressive education program to feel that they were better than everyone else. People constantly called them "gifted" or "talented." As a result, they resented having to be so close to that other school—God forbid a passerby might mix them up with someone in special education, those kids who were whispered about with pitiful sighs and insincere condolences. Still, the kids in the progressive program ended up mingling with many of the special-ed students. My favorite was Scott. He was always smiling. His hair stuck up in the air and it didn't look like a comb ever touched it. He was twelve and he had Down's syndrome and a voice as low as a blues singer's. He walked like a caveman and had no complexes about being different. He shook hands and gave high fives and often didn't realize that when kids laughed, they were laughing at him, so he joined right in with them. I told them to knock it off a few times.

After school, as he waited for the bus, Scott would munch on potato chips and sip from a can of soda. If he caught sight of me, he'd yell my name across the street, wanting to share his snack with me. Once a wiseguy from my class named Malcolm knocked the can from his hand and then said he was sorry in a haughty tone. David grabbed my arm as he anticipated my next move, which would have been to break Malcolm's face. But Scott showed us all. He reached into his backpack and took out another can. Before opening it, he held it out to Malcolm and said that he would split it with him. Malcolm shook his hand and apologized. Scott smiled and continued to wait for his bus. I thought about that gesture for days. Maybe the meek *will* inherit the earth.

Spring also brought baseball season, and that always put me in the best mood. I had visions every year of the Yankees making it to the World Series, and I tried to follow every game. My favorite player was Don Mattingly. David, who thought that I was a step away from the funny farm because I got so obsessed with the Yankees' performance, would say to me, "There are a hundred things wrong in your life, and you're worried about the Yankees winning a doubleheader?"

For sure. There was nothing I could do about the bad situation at home. Rough things would happen there whether I was miserable or having a good time, so I chose the latter. Scott was a Yankees fan too, and sometimes he ran after me in the schoolyard to give me a play-by-play of the game from the night before. It didn't help to tell him that I already knew everything that had happened, because he would have continued talking anyway. Sometimes he cut out articles from the newspaper and brought them to me, and he always gave me the doubles to his baseball cards. When we played ball during lunch break, he begged to get a chance at bat. Sometimes the guys would let him, but at other times they'd shoo him over to his own side of the schoolyard. He cried once, so I told him that he could take my turn at bat—defying anyone to argue with me. He could hit, too, and I'd laugh as he ran around the bases cheering for himself. He declared me his best friend and hugged me in the most unashamed manner. I envied his purity—his trust of his own feelings. Some of my classmates tried to give me the business by saying that people were going to mistake me for special ed. "I'll be in great company," I responded. We were supposed to be the smart ones—the future leaders of America. It's amazing the way unkindness always manages to become part of the agenda. I had no patience for it—wanted no part of it.

Mr. Pierson, the vice-principal of my school, had put together a team that would play twice a week after school against public schools from other districts. Several people didn't sign up because they hated Mr. Pierson. He was actually known to snarl at people when they made him angry, and therefore he was given the nickname

"Dogface." They said he was mean and vicious and it was bad enough having to deal with him during school hours—so to be around him after school was just added hassle. I wanted so much to play that you could have told me Hitler was the coach and I would have joined. The truth was, I had never had a confrontation with Mr. Pierson. He nodded and said good morning when I walked past him into the building. He rather amused me sometimes because he tried too hard to be cool. His clothes and hairstyle were always picture-perfect. He didn't walk, he swaggered, and he had a shrill, piercing voice when he yelled. He wanted everyone to hear him. That had no effect on me one way or another as long as I stayed out of his way, so I reasoned that if he was to be my vehicle for joining the baseball team, so be it. I was signing up. The problem was that he had already posted his sign-up sheet and taken it down. I hadn't had a chance to sign it. The guys said that it meant he had enough players already. The first game would be played against a school in the South Bronx.

I told David and Billy that I was going to talk to him anyway and ask if he would make an exception.

Billy shook his head. "Don't do it, Tone, you know how good old Dogface is—he'll get his jollies telling you that you should have signed up and he won't let you play anyway."

David figured that if I caught him in the right

mood and kissed his butt enough, he would say all right. I decided against it. I wanted to play, but I didn't want everything that I did to be such an effort. I had this picture in my mind that you show up at a field and get into a game. That's what made it so wholesome—that's what made baseball so great to me. It had nothing to do with getting into anyone's good graces. I didn't mind that Mr. Pierson was going to be the coach, but I did very much mind having to suck up to him.

Still, I agonized for three days whether or not I should approach Mr. Pierson. Each time I even came close to it, I chickened out because I had already made up my mind that he would say no. We had even had occasion to talk to each other when I helped him put test booklets together in the office. We worked silently for a half hour speaking only to say where the books went. As I dusted my hand off on my pants, our eyes met and he smiled. It was a kind smile, too.

"Is there anything I can do for you?" he asked.

Now was my chance. I swallowed hard and said, "Can I have a pass back to class?"

David later shook his head and told me that I was crazy. "You had your chance, you idiot! Why didn't you ask him?"

My friend didn't realize how angry I was at myself, and didn't expect me to blow up at him. "Because I didn't want him to say no, all right?"

"Hey, Tone—we don't need Pierson to play a good game of ball. Forget it."

"I forgot it!" I shouted as I headed for my class, leaving him to wonder if I had finally lost my mind.

As I sat through my next class, Ms. Marks—one of my favorite teachers—noticed that tears were falling more quickly than I could wipe them away, and called me out in the hall under the guise of taking a message to the office.

"Do you need a pass to the nurse or the men's room?" she asked.

I sucked in a breath and shook my head.

"Would you like to take a walk around the building?"

I shook my head again.

She smiled. "Okay, Tony, this is your lucky day. If I could grant you a wish, what would it be?" I shrugged. "Come on, humor me," she said.

"It would be to play baseball." Tears began to fall again, and I tried to bolt away from her. She grabbed my arm and asked me to wait a minute. "Ms. Marks, I'm just tired," I pleaded. "Can't I just go wash my face and come back to class?"

"Yeah, you can," she said softly, "if you take a minute and calm down." I agreed to do that. "Okay, let's be logical here." I nodded. "Something's eating at you—I know you well enough to know that. Obviously, you don't want to talk about it—so would you do me a favor?"

"Okay," I answered as I wiped my eyes.

"Would you rethink what's got you so upset

and ask yourself whether you're making the right choices about the situation?"

That seemed fair—actually, it seemed smart—so I promised I would. She excused me from class and suggested I go down to the nurse's office to lie down until the next class period. She gave me a note and a hug and said that my homework assignment was to see about that baseball game. As I lay on that cot in the nurse's office, drifting in and out of sleep, I thought about how complicated things were—and how complicated I made them. I had this habit of wanting things to fall right into place, and got angry when they didn't. The situation at home was a given—nothing good would happen there—but school was different. It was the only place where I relaxed, felt cared about, and had a good time. People smiled at me, knew my name, even respected me. I wanted to keep things that way, and it occurred to me, as I drifted off into what wound up being a two-hour nap, that this was my responsibility.

Coincidentally, Mr. Pierson was the person who woke me and asked whether I needed for someone to come and take me home. I shook my head immediately and squinted at the clock on the wall. It was already time to leave. I prayed that a note would not be sent home about my not getting enough rest. He asked whether something hurt, and said he was concerned because it took so long to get me awake.

"I'm all right, Mr. Pierson," I assured him as

I threw off the blanket that was on me. "I guess I got too relaxed."

He smiled as he extended a hand to help me to sit up. He told me to take it easy for the rest of the day. As he turned to leave, I called out his name and asked if I could talk to him. He came and sat down next to me.

"Mr. Pierson," I began slowly, "I hadn't realized that you posted the sign-up sheet for the baseball team and I didn't join. I was wondering if, well, maybe you'll need an extra guy—I'd really like to play."

He stared at me for a moment, and I panicked. Sure, he was going to tell me that if I was dumb enough not to have signed up, it was too late now. Besides, I'd slept all afternoon and now I wanted to play ball?

"Be in the park in an hour and you can play."

I thought I'd heard wrong. "Excuse me?"

"The game is at four, make sure you're there."

"Thanks, Mr. Pierson," I called out as I ran down the hall and headed for the locker. Ms. Marks intercepted me and asked where I was going in such a hurry. "To do your homework assignment," I said as she smiled and told me to have a good time.

I did have a good time, too. Mr. Pierson, it turned out, really knew his baseball. He coached us in fielding and hitting. He encouraged us and let us try again when we messed up. He clapped heartily when we got hits and slid into bases. What I liked best was that he stressed that we were there to have a good time. There was a cooler on our side of the bleachers filled with Gatorade, and he told us to help ourselves. When other teams got rowdy over plays or the umpire's calls, he was the one who managed to calm everyone down. It was old Dogface who taught me how to choke up on the bat and to switch-hit. When I had mastered it, he was as happy as I was. Once when I ripped my T-shirt he told me to take one out of his duffel bag. After the games I would help him to gather the equipment and place it in his car. He'd thank me, I'd tell him that I'd had a great time, and then I'd rush off to join David. I would have loved to hang out and talk to Mr. Pierson and let him know who the real me was—apart from that shy person I usually seemed to be, but that was definitely against the rules. If he knew too much, he would want to help me. There would be no way that he could—and I'd lose what I already had and very much wanted to keep.

Scott took to coming to the field every day, making himself available to pick up bats and balls, hand out towels, pour drinks, and even sweep home plate. Every time someone made a hit, he cheered until he was hoarse. When people struck out or hit into a fly ball, he assured them that their next turn would give them the big hit. It was apparent that he knew the rules of baseball. Mr. Pierson grinned a few times when Scott would emphatically declare "ground rule double" or "pitch-out." He was *always* right.

One afternoon he approached Mr. Pierson and asked to be put in the game, promising that he would do his best. Mr. Pierson smiled and placed an affectionate arm around his shoulder. He told him that he knew he would, and sent him to cover first base, whereupon Donny threw down his glove and said that it wasn't fair.

"Oh, I see," said Mr. Pierson. "But it was fair for him to get you towels when you were sweating?" Donny stared at the ground. "I think you need to take a long hard look at your sense of justice." He turned and addressed the team. "I want you to tell me what the right thing to do is. I want you to tell me if you feel all right to tell Scott that he has to leave because he happens to go to a different school."

Donny knew better than to open his mouth again. Mr. Pierson had made it clear that this wasn't the major leagues and we were there to get some fresh air and exercise. He reminded everyone to think about the last time they felt left out of something. Although I didn't say anything, I agreed with him. Why should the place where Scott went to school determine whether or not he should be allowed to play baseball? From that day on, Scott was the first one at the field, smiling from ear to ear as he stood leaning on his bat. Even the guys who complained about him at first were grinning at his enthusiasm and persistence. No one was as happy as he was just to be a part of things. Those who protested were forced to admit that he was a damn good player.

He bailed the team out of the hole more than once. Winning and losing had nothing to do with it, either. He was just having the time of his life. We all could have taken a lesson from him.

During our last game of the season, our opponents had targeted Scott as an object of ridicule from the first inning. They laughed because he nodded his head constantly at the signals and because he cheered so much. One of their players tripped as Scott reached down to tag him out at first. Scott immediately apologized and extended a hand to help him up. He pushed Scott and called him a retard—causing me to leave my position at shortstop and run after him. Mr. Pierson, who also had seen what happened, sent me back to the field and said that we needed to get on with the game—a game that we won 13–3.

When it was over, Mr. Pierson pulled me aside and told me it was a nice thing that I'd wanted to do for Scott. I asked why he didn't let me.

"We've got to let people do what they need to do," he answered. "I see lots of things that people don't realize I see. Like I see that you're a very sensitive guy." I made a face. "How many times did you let Scott take your turn in the schoolyard? Yeah, I saw—and I saw you help him to grease his glove—most of all, I saw how much it didn't disturb you to let him play. The thing is, in order to let Scott be one of the guys, we have to let him fight his own battles."

"What if he couldn't?" I asked.

"We always find a way to survive, don't we?"

I nodded and swallowed hard. He knew there was much more to me than I revealed. He put his arm around my shoulder. "You've got a heart that's going to lead you to the right places. Everything will fall in place when that happens. You'll see." I put the equipment in his trunk and thanked him for a great baseball season. We shook hands and he drove off. You'd think I could have said something more important to this person who had played a key role in helping me to get a positive grasp on myself, but I couldn't. I was afraid of what that truth would make me feel.

Two months later, budget cuts reassigned Mr. Pierson to a school across town, and Scott was sent to a vocational school in Long Island. That was the same month I decided to make a move and dialed the hot-line number that put me in touch with Pop. I've since realized that baseball, the game that I love so much, is riddled with scandals, ambitious owners, and disputes over multimillion-dollar contracts. Not so wholesome after all. But there are those who'd play just because they love the game. I'm one of them.

I'd like to be able to tell Dogface that my heart had led me to the right place. I'd like to tell him that those days on the baseball field were memorable—that they made the horrors of reality bearable. I miss Scott and often think about him chasing me down with box scores from the *Daily News*. I wonder if he remembers me, and if he still loves the Yankees so much. There is truth in the poem written by the late baseball commissioner A. Bartlett Giamatti about baseball—that it is designed "to break your heart" because when you turn around, it's over. So you have to cherish each moment. Scott's cheers taught me that. So did the quiet kindness of the man we called Dogface.

# And to All a Good Night

Every year without warning I stumbled over Christmas. I always reassured myself that I would be better prepared when the next one rolled around, but it never happened. Once I got past Halloween, Thanksgiving was upon me and then Christmas, just a short time away. Holidays represented things I had to lie about and reminded me that my life wasn't the way I wanted it to be.

David felt the same way I did. He resented the fact that beautiful music and talk of peace on earth and goodwill toward men wasn't a yearlong thing. Why, he argued, were Thanksgiving and Christmas the only times to remember that people needed baskets of food and presents? "Besides," he said, "did you ever get a good look at the garbage that gets thrown into those baskets? People get more canned beans and macaroni and cheese than they want to see for the rest of their lives. Why the hell don't they hold a toy drive in April or May? Kids need things to play with during those months, too."

"It's better than nothing," I argued. "At least during this season people take some time to be nice to one another."

He wasn't convinced, and he paraphrased Ebenezer Scrooge without even knowing it. David had never read *A Christmas Carol*, but Scrooge's outlook summed up his attitude toward the season. David said that it was a great excuse for people to spend a whole lot of money they didn't have, and while Christmas might keep the misery of the world at bay for a few weeks, the letdown when it was all over wasn't worth it.

It was one Christmas Eve when his mother left David with twenty dollars, two boxes of Cheerios, six microwave dinners, a strip of candy canes, and a note telling him to have a Merry Christmas, when the truth came out about why he hated the holidays so much. At the time his mother was dating a tour-bus driver who made trips back and forth from New York to Florida. She decided to join him for Christmas. David threw a cereal box so hard against the wall that he dented its side.

"I don't expect anything from her, Tone, and she never disappoints me, either." Tears formed in his eyes as he sat down at the kitchen table and reread his mother's note. Taking the strip of candy canes, he began to smash them with his thumb. I ripped one from the batch and did the same thing. Our eyes met and I shrugged, as I always did to emphasize to him that it was best to forget about something. We threw the candy canes aside, and, although he pretended to be reading the instructions for the microwave dinners, I knew that his insides were seething. He had learned the hard way that to want anything would cause him pain and get him into trouble, but Christmas had a way of bringing a glimmer of hope that wanting was all right to do.

We cooked all the microwave dinners, dumping them into a large bowl that the two of us picked from like an elaborate buffet. Despite David's adamant protests, I found one of those instrumental music stations on the radio and we ate to the tune of "God Rest Ye Merry Gentlemen" and exchanged Christmas horror stories.

When he was four years old, David's father had promised to take him to see Santa at Macy's if he would first let his father sleep late in the morning. There was a woman spending the night with him and he wanted David to make himself scarce. Three-thirty in the afternoon rolled around and his father showed no signs of getting up. David was afraid that if he didn't get to see Santa before Christmas Eve, he might not get the bike he wanted. Each time during the year that he'd asked his father for one, he was told to wait for Santa. This was his last chance. At five-fifteen, desperate to get to Macy's, David opened the door to the bedroom and found his father and his companion smoking dope and drinking.

"What do you want?" his father asked him nastily. David reminded him of his promise, and his father reached over and slapped him across the head. "There ain't no damn Santa! There's just a white man they pay to make brats like you ask for things that they don't deserve!" David was thrown out of the room and went into the kitchen, where he ate half a loaf of bread with mustard. He never got the bike—Christmas went unnoticed altogether. There was never a tree, a big dinner, or any gifts to open. David went to bed that night and realized that his father was right about Santa. He was afraid because the world was so scary. Now David agreed with me that it was a relief not to have someone hanging threats over your head in order for you to get things that you want.

Such was my case. My parents always told me that Santa wouldn't come for me because I was a "bad boy." I even received a note stating that I got nothing for that reason. Every picture I ever saw of Santa, he was happy and he smiled. I thought of him seeing me when I was sleeping and knowing when I was bad or good, and it unnerved me. When I was in the second grade, one of my classmates talked about how he spied on his mother when she took packages from the closet and placed them underneath the Christmas tree. He said that she later admitted to him that Santa Claus was just made up. I was so relieved—the only thing I had to contend with was the usual feeling that I wasn't like the other kids. Given my circumstances at home, Santa Claus served only as a great source of paranoia.

Because of our track record with Christmas, David and I began our own individual rituals to get through the season. As we complained that afternoon about being too stuffed from our makeshift banquet, we decided that we needed our own way of making the season bright. We thought about what would make us happiest, and David told me about how his mother had talked about getting him a tree.

"She asked what I wanted, Tone. It ain't like I asked her for a damn thing! I said that a tree might be nice." He kicked the chair. "She's nobody's fool. She figured that Florida would be better."

"You've got twenty bucks. Let's go see how much one costs," I suggested.

"What are we going to do with it?" He scowled.

"We can bring it back here and decorate it."

"With what?"

"We can decide that later."

It took some persuasion, but David agreed and we headed over to Columbus Avenue, where two brothers named Andy and Roy were unloading all sizes and shapes of trees from the back of their pickup truck. We offered to help. They thanked us and told us to stand the small trees up against the walls of the surrounding stores. We realized immediately that we couldn't afford their trees because even the small, puny Charlie Brown–looking ones were thirty dollars and up. We were having a good time, though. They let us sit on the side of their truck as they stood around and sold their trees. They had a tape player with Christmas music going, and they kept wishing everyone a Merry Christmas. Roy made some wreaths and taught us how to tie them together. We went and got them coffee and doughnuts and they insisted we get some for ourselves.

Andy and Roy were teachers from upstate New York who had a few acres of land. Every Christmas Eve they came into the city for the day to sell trees, because it gave them a chance to earn some extra money and to get a feel of Christmas in New York. We noticed the way they almost always allowed themselves to be talked down from their original prices. A young couple with a baby in a stroller took a long time to pick a tree and then decided on a five-foot-tall evergreen. They knew exactly which corner of their apartment the tree would go in, and they imagined themselves standing in front of it to pose for pictures. They easily persuaded the brothers to accept ten dollars less for it. The same went for an elderly couple who smiled and talked about how wonderful the fir smelled. Men in suits took the ten-footers and had no time to negotiate prices. David and I got ten dollars for tying one down to the roof of a station wagon. A priest bought a full evergreen for a church altar, and a young mother with three children took a six-foot-tall fir.

Each time a sale was made, a sad smile crossed David's lips. The faraway look on his face was obvious to whoever looked at him. Andy began to talk to him, to ask him to move trees and to go for sandwiches. I could tell he knew that David was feeling a lot and he wanted to help.

Two boys about our age came to price a wreath, taking the time to count the crumpled bills and assorted change that came from the taller one's pocket. They stepped over to the side and agreed that they could afford the wreath if they walked where they were going and only took the subway home. They turned back to us, smiled, and told Roy they would take it.

"What are you guys going to do with it?" he asked.

"We're putting it on our mother's grave."

Roy handed it to them. "Merry Christmas. Say an extra prayer for us this year." The boys shook their hands and said thank-you.

"How do you know that wasn't staged?" David asked cynically as they walked away.

"It didn't feel staged," Roy replied, "and if it was, shame on them, not me."

After several hours, all but two of the small trees had been sold and the brothers were getting ready to head back home. They thanked us for the company and asked us to write them from time to time. They had scrawled their addresses on the back of a brown paper bag with hot chocolate stains on it. We shook hands with them, wished them a Merry Christmas, and started away when Andy called to David, "Why don't you find someone who can use this tree? I doubt we'll sell it." David smiled and, behind his back, I nodded and mouthed Andy a thank-you.

We rushed to David's house with the tree, where we decorated it with paper chains and loose-leaf balls that we crumpled up and attached with his mother's bobby pins. We got a pizza and two milk shakes, and when the Yule log came on the TV we invented our gift game. We cut up strips of paper and wrote down gifts that we would give each other. He gave me a baseball jacket, Reeboks, and a gift certificate to a bookstore. I gave him a drafting kit, two three-piece suits, and dinner at Leo Lindy's.

It was around four in the morning when we fell asleep underneath an afghan on opposite ends of the couch. Our gifts were around us, an empty pizza box was on the floor in front of us, and all our love and good wishes surrounded us as we took comfort in the sorry-looking tree standing lopsided in a bucket.

We lost touch with Andy and Roy because they stopped writing, but we did manage to keep up our gift-giving tradition even when the two of us wound up in better homes. As I write this, Christmas is upon me again. There's still not peace on earth, and Charlie Brown's dread of Christmas being too commercial is still a legitimate concern. On the other hand, small miracles do occur, and remind us that the biggest miracle happened thousands of years ago—in a cold barn.

# Be Careful What You Wish For

When I moved in with Mom and Pop, the transition period in my life had begun, and it was a relief. They'd made it clear during the time I spent in the hospital that I was no longer on my own. They were to be my parents, which meant that they would look out for me. They were going to take care of me. Unlike before, when I was hungry, Mom was ready with a meal. My clothes were plentiful and always clean. There was no fear in the night because the only thing that anyone did here was sleep. There were toys around the house, the refrigerator was loaded with food, and the air was filled with laughter. Problems were handled as a family—nothing was too big. I'd never heard of such a thing as a family meeting. I was in awe for the first few weeks at just how much love was a part of this household. No one hit anyone else or raised his or her voice. There were good-night kisses followed by "I love you" and "Sleep with the angels." There was no question that would not be answered, no topic too difficult to discuss.

I smiled one evening as I caught myself staring at Robin snuggling next to Mom while they lay on the couch together. Mom hugged and kissed her and rubbed her head. It was obvious that they were enjoying this moment. I knew I could get used to these things quite easily.

Mom would always hear me when I stirred in the middle of the night. She'd come into my room and stand next to my bed. Sometimes she'd ask if I wanted anything, and other times she would quietly stroke my head until I fell back to sleep. She realized that it was hard for me to help myself to food, so she took to leaving oranges in my bedroom for me so that I would have snacks on hand when I wanted them. She knew that I had trouble accepting things, but figured I would eat them if they were there and no one was watching me. At first I had trouble eating them, but then I realized that as the bowl emptied she kept refilling it.

This all was a dream come true. Everything I had heard about what it could be like to be happy was true. These were people who lived from one day to the next doing whatever the day called for and making the best of whatever that was. There was no room for harm, only for love. It's not that this was a "Leave It to Beaver" life where everything was swell and parents cleaned the house with big wide smiles and came to the table dressed to go to a cocktail party, but it was very real. Sometimes Pop got annoyed when the girls and I messed around too much at the table or when we had the TV on too loud. Mom threatened to hang us from the clothesline if we didn't keep our rooms clean, and we often made faces about it. But we felt very safe and secure in the fact that there were no threats—no one would ever hurt anyone else here. The love around us allowed for the bad moods and the occasional mishaps. That love would help get us through a hard time.

David never trusted the intentions or the sincerity of these people I had become so fond of. He said that it all sounded too damn good to be true, and that this new life was just a disaster waiting to happen. He accused me for the thousandth time of being naive, and wanted to know what it was going to take for me to understand that the world was mean and cruel. He didn't want me calling these people Mom and Pop. He feared that this investment of trust and emotion would blow up in my face. "Figure out why they're being so nice to you, Tone," he said. "Nobody does that." He didn't want to hear that they had not given me reason to be suspicious, because he was positive that in due time they would. He thought the two of us should take off together and make our way by ourselves.

My loyalty was torn between my new family and my best friend. I wanted them to like each other—I wanted David to realize that this was not like before, and that he didn't have to keep the wolves away from me. I hoped that in time he would understand this was not a place that I wanted to leave, and that I wanted him to be just as much a part of my life here.

It got to be a real problem when David refused to accept the fact that we didn't have to run scared anymore. He asked me to meet him one night to ride trains, and I agreed because it was important for David to see that I didn't want anything to change between us. We'd always done that, and I was feeling pretty good and saw no reason why I should refuse. As I was to find out, there were two reasons: Mom and Pop. They said it was out of the question, that there was no way I was going to ride trains until all hours of the night.

Pop launched into a heated tirade. "I don't know whether or not you've lost your mind, but I'll sure be the one to help you find it."

"Wait a minute," I argued. "David is my best friend. Why should that change just because I live here?"

"We're not asking you to change anything," Pop stated matter-of-factly, his face indicating that he wasn't at all intimidated by my tough attitude. "We're just telling you that you're not riding in the underground jungle. Let David come here if you want to hang out."

Mom agreed. "He can spend the weekend and I'll make plenty of snacks. There's just no reason to run off like that anymore. You have a home."

I finally agreed to that after Pop made it clear

that there would be no discussion about riding trains. He didn't care a damn what I'd done before—I wasn't doing it anymore.

We drove into Times Square to pick David up. The whole time Pop kept declaring that steel bars should be built around Times Square—they should lock up the place and throw the keys away. He shook his head in disbelief at the pace, the audacity, and the overall attitude of the people around us. I just smiled at him, amused because the whole atmosphere made him crazy. We found David in Playland, an arcade with rows of video games and people peddling their drugs and their bodies. Pop honked the horn when we spotted him.

"What in the *hell* would he want to hang in a place like that for?" Pop asked as he became impatient to leave.

I shrugged. "I don't know, Pop. I enjoyed myself when I hung in there."

"Well, Tony-Bob," he retorted as he shook his head again, "you're not going to be enjoying it anymore."

"Why not?" David asked as he took his place in the backseat.

Pop started the car. "Because that place is a hellhole and you guys got no business being in there."

Although no more was said about Playland once we got back to the house, I could tell that David was annoyed, so I called him on it.

"I saw you making a face at my Pop. Why did you do that?"

He waved his hand at me and rolled his eyes. "Why do you let these people tell you what to do?" he asked angrily. "You've got to be crazy. What are they holding on you?"

For a moment I said nothing, and then I waited until he looked at me. "I love them, David."

I didn't expect the explosion that followed. "Now I believe that you have truly wacked out! You love them? Tony, listen to yourself!"

"I *have* listened to myself," I argued. "That's how I know that I love them. They've been good to me. Look around this room. Look at these clothes I'm wearing, the food we ate tonight. It didn't come from the tooth fairy."

"Sooner or later, Tone, they're going to want something for it. Do you have what it costs to pay for it?"

I shook my head adamantly. "It's not about that here. We love and respect each other. No one does that kind of stuff."

David made a face when he realized that Pop had come to the door of my bedroom. "No one has yet."

"Do you guys want to take a ride to Pizza Hut? The girls are having pizza cravings."

I shook my head. "No thanks, Pop, we'll hang here and find something to do."

David mimicked Pop when he told us to have a good time.

"Cut it out, David," I said. "You don't have to do that."

David shoved me and told me to get out of his way. He began to collect his clothes and declared that he was leaving. He refused, he said, to stay in prison and be told what to do by some has-been drill sergeant.

"That's not fair, David. You've never talked to him. Why can't you give him a chance? He's been good to me."

"And he's trying to own you!"

I shook my head as I begged him to listen to me. "You always got so mad when anyone hurt me. Here I am with two people who'll do whatever it takes to make me feel good, to feel human, and you're mad. He loves me, David. Don't you understand that? All that time when I was sick, those two people never left my side. They got me everything I needed—and things that I wanted. They adopted me—made me their son, protected me from every harm that came in my direction. Why are you opposed to that?"

"Because the punchline will be here soon. You're going to get it through your head someday that there is no such thing as Santa Claus."

"Well, then, why do so many people wait for him?"

"Because they're too stupid to know any better." David shoved me aside again and said that he was leaving. "If you were smart, you'd go with me."

We argued for ten more minutes as I stubbornly declared that Mom and Pop weren't taking over my life. Finally he said, "If you truly believe that, prove it to me. Come with me to Playland. The old Tone would have never fought me on this. He would have just gone."

David and I were on our way to Playland in fifteen minutes. I had to show him that nothing had changed between us. I had to make him understand that my life was better and he didn't have to watch out so much for me anymore. Yet it didn't feel right that I was being forced to prove something that was so obviously in my heart. I had never had to do that with David before. If anything, he always trusted my feelings, though he rarely agreed with them.

We were both more than surprised to see Pop standing at the door of the arcade an hour later. David shrugged and turned away. I just stood still. I knew that Pop could read the look of shock on my face. I wondered how I could explain the conflict within me.

"Get in the car right now," he said evenly. I turned to look for David. "I said now, Tony." His face warned that he was not in the mood to be disobeyed. I walked ahead of him and heard as he called to David. "You too, David. Let's go."

David wasn't budging. "You can't tell me what to do."

"Get in the car, David, or I'll yank you by the seat of your pants out this door."

Amazingly, David obeyed him and stormed out the door ahead of me, cursing under his breath.

Pop caught up with me as we got outside, and our eyes met. David turned around, positioning himself to jump on Pop if he did anything to me.

"Do you realize that you scared the hell out of your mama and me?" I shook my head. "I know that you know better, Tony. What was in your head to do this?"

"I asked him to come!" David declared, ready for a good fight.

Pop wasn't the least bit affected by his bad-ass routine. "I see that you weren't using your head either." Pop shook his head. "Get in the car and let's get back. Your mama is worried sick."

"Well, Tone, this is where I say good-bye," David said.

Pop could have blown up, backhanded me, or threatened to put me through a wall. But he didn't do any of those things. A kind look crossed his face and he rubbed my back. It was then I knew that the light bulb had gone off in his head and he understood how I was being pulled in every direction. He understood that I loved him and Mom, but that I loved David too. He winked and told me to get in the car. Then he pulled David aside and they talked for close to ten minutes. At last David got into the car and sat next to me. He didn't seem so angry. He even turned and smiled at me twice and told Pop of a short-cut to get out of town. When we got back to the house, he joined me in apologizing to Mom. I didn't know what had gone on between David and Pop, but I knew I loved Pop so much—more than I'd even realized till then. I didn't have to say anything, but he knew—love did that. His for me, and mine for him.

Later that night, no longer able to contain my curiosity, I asked David what Pop had said to him when they were outside Playland.

"He said enough to let me know that you're safe. I've been pretty rude to those guys because I didn't want you to get set up to be hurt. They won't hurt you, Tone, so make sure you don't ruin a good thing."

Suddenly I began to cry, and he jumped off of his chair and came over to me. "What are you doing that for? Come on, Tone, cut it out!"

"I'm all right," I tried to assure him. "It's just that I wouldn't be able to stand it if you walked away."

David slapped my head. "All of those crazy books you read have begun to affect your brain. That never would have happened, you idiot! It never will happen. Now cut it out, I hate this kind of crap."

After David fell asleep, I lay awake for a long time and thought about the events of the last few months. Everything that was happening was exactly what I wanted to be happening. As I lay in the dark and marveled at the wonder that the realization of my dream had brought, I began to get frightened. Was this what I truly wanted? There was no question that I was happy—I didn't think I was as well equipped as I'd been before for a good fight. It was as if I was tired and wound down. I got up and sat in the living room and was so deep in thought that Pop startled me when he came and sat next to me. He cupped his hand over the back of my head.

"What's the matter, son? Can't you sleep?" I shook my head and moved closer to him. "It's pretty scary, isn't it?"

"What's pretty scary?" I asked without looking up at him.

"Getting what you asked for—what you wished for." I shrugged and he went on, "Sometimes things change and we're not sure whether we've been true to our wishes and dreams all the time that we held on so tight to them."

"Pop, it's just that I keep thinking about things that I want to hold on to." I told him about feeling too tired to fight, and that David was just about the only thing that I did want to hold on to.

He nodded his head and pulled me onto his lap. "Tony-Bob, there's no reason for you to fight anymore. That's what you've got your mama and me for. We'll do it for you. As for your friendship with David—you and David are lifers. That means there is nothing—not even death—that could separate your hearts. That would be true no matter where either of you were. Anyone who tries to interfere with that is just plain crazy."

I turned my head and looked at his face. "You told him that today, didn't you, Pop?" I reached up to hug him and laid my head on his shoulder. "Thanks."

"There's no reason to thank me, son. David has been very good to you. I think the world of him for that. I respect him." He hugged me tight and then he said, "And I'll yank the skin off your behind if I ever have to go and get you out of that hellhole again."

We stayed up a little while and ate the leftover pizza. Pop talked about friendship and love and how vital those things were if one wanted to make it in this crazy world. He told me about guys in Stamps that he still visited, how they always treated one another as if no time had gone by since the last visit. They laughed about things that they did, and were as proud as peacocks of their accomplishments, their families, and their lives. I tried to imagine sitting around with David, both of us gray, wrinkled, and with a spare tire around the middle. I wondered how many kids we would have, what the futures that we so looked forward to would become. An hour later, when I closed my eyes to sleep, I felt so peaceful.

That feeling was all I ever wanted.

# See Farthest,
# Fly Higher

If anyone could have seen the manic way I ran around my bedroom and packed my suitcase to go on vacation with Mom, Pop, and the girls, they would have laughed and realized that it was the first of my life. If I had to write a back-to-school composition about my summer, this one would be honest. The trip promised to bring me back into contact with my peers, and I welcomed even the obnoxious ones. Throughout the entire drive to Connecticut I was silly, excited, and never stopped talking. Pop said he was going to gag me with a road map as he smiled at me in the rearview mirror. When we stopped for lunch, he took me aside and asked, "So how does it feel to be on your first vacation?" My eyes filled with tears and he hugged me. "Don't worry, son, there will be plenty more."

We rented a log cabin with four rooms—two on each side. There was a well behind it for water, and a canal nearby. The nights were cool enough for blankets and the days were warm enough for getting a suntan. It was not unusual to wake up at dawn and find a deer family drinking from the canal. After a week of trying, I managed to get a picture of them with Mom's zoom lens.

In no time I got accustomed to being on vacation. It was a luxury to sit under trees, swim until my skin shriveled, and not have to worry about any set schedule. Since my uncles, aunts, and cousins were staying in adjoining cabins, there was always plenty of company. We could improvise ball games at a moment's notice. When the younger kids went to sleep, I stayed outside until I got sleepy enough to go to bed. Sometimes the men played poker on a card table. I'd pull a folding chair next to Pop's and lay my head against his arm to be able to see his cards and play his hand silently. It was amusing to see how seriously they took these games. They played a nickel a point, and the winners never came away with more than ten or fifteen bucks, but an onlooker would think this was a Las Vegas tournament. It was a blast to watch the brothers as they insulted one another and threw the cards down in disgust, and to hear Pop's "I'll be damned," declared so adamantly in his Southern drawl. The most fun, though, came whenever they sat around and talked. My uncles are terrific storytellers, and they have wonderful senses of humor. They all have the same hearty laugh, and love to play practical jokes on one another.

Surprisingly, I didn't miss New York for a minute. A lot happened to me in the course of the summer. Besides being able to settle in comfortably with a family that I had come to relax with and enjoy so much, I learned a great deal more about myself. Some of the lessons were as hard to swallow as honey and maple syrup combined.

Every afternoon, kids would congregate at the lake a quarter of a mile away from the cabin. Most of them went to boarding schools and had parents who were very wealthy and oblivious to their activities. Those kids were very sophisticated and worldly—they dropped lines about going to London or Paris as if they were talking about walking to the corner store. They wore designer clothes and got hairstyles as opposed to haircuts. They had credit cards and paid for sodas with twenty-dollar bills. While not one of them was over sixteen years old, they all had some kind of sexual experiences. Drinking and smoking were old hat, as were marijuana, cocaine, and pills. Unlike the kids in New York, who usually resorted to the less expensive attractions like crack and Night Train Express, these kids could afford to buy the "good stuff." Some talked about how their parents used it at parties.

The first clue I got that I "wasn't in Kansas anymore" was on the first day, when I got into a fight with a preppie who was masquerading as a biker-in-training for the summer. His name was "Slick." He was sixteen and crude. He began to make lewd and smutty remarks at my sister Robin, who was playing Barbie dolls under a tree with some other little girls. He said that her hair, which was waist-length and dark, made him horny. I dug my fingers into his shoulder and said, "She's ten years old, can't you do better?"

He returned my glare and asked what business of mine it was. I pointed to both Robin and Gina. "Those two—they're totally off limits to you."

Slick laughed mockingly and tried to get his friends to join in. Then, without warning, he walked up behind Robin and tugged at the back of her shorts. Like a nuclear reaction, I drew my right hand back, made a fist, and, giving it everything I had, landed it across his nose. When he tried to hit back, I punched him again and aimed a threatening look at one of his friends who moved as though to intervene. As his nose gushed with blood, I repeated between labored breaths, "Those two are off limits."

In a last-ditch effort to preserve his dignity, Slick said, "My brother is twice your size and would kick your ass in a heartbeat."

I nodded confidently as I motioned with my hand and said, between breaths, "Bring him on."

I went back to the cabin and threw up for a

half hour. Part of my nausea came from amazement that I hadn't gotten myself killed. There was so much more to it, though. Exhaustion overcame me as I realized all too well that Pop was right—a good fight was sometimes the only way to drive a point home. This wasn't my first fight and it sure wouldn't be my last, but I felt uneasy on such strange turf. This wasn't like having a fight on the streets of New York. There was something unfamiliar here, something acutely foreign, and I knew that I would never feel totally comfortable. I wondered if I was cut out for civilization.

Slick began to circulate rumors about me. He told people that I was an insane product of the New York streets and that they needed to watch out for me because I could fly off the handle and become dangerous. He warned my unsuspecting potential victims that I probably hung around with gang members. Gina came home one day and announced that Slick had said I'd gotten my limp in a fight with a cop in New York, when he shot me in the leg. How cool, I thought; it almost made having a stroke worthwhile. Pop, amused by it all, advised me to sit back and say nothing. To acknowledge the story as truth would make me seem cocky. To deny it would invite more rumors.

To Slick's chagrin, whatever his slanderous intentions were, they backfired, and the older guys were coming around and introducing themselves to me. Girls flirted and hinted about dates. As I semi-mingled with the "privileged" class, I became frightfully aware that the name of the game was acceptance. Either you were accepted or you weren't. What was scary and made me a little ashamed was the reality that even though I wasn't at all crazy about this crowd, I gloated over their deference toward me. Though I harbored my own private antagonisms toward them, my presence was obvious and I included myself in every conversation, though I was guarded enough not to reveal very much about myself. Unlike the kinship I had treasured with my New York schoolmates David, Billy, Denise, and Allison, this group and I shared nothing in common. Their lives revolved around their sexual conquests. The competitive edge was fierce as they struggled to see how long and by what ingenious method they could get someone to "do it" with them. I hated the categorization of first, second, and third base, and felt rattled when someone referred to "getting a piece."

My hormones were just as active as theirs were. It scared me to death, though, to follow along with their serious pursuit of sex. It meant that I would have to act in a way that I neither knew how nor wanted to. I had seen sex in its basest form within the imprisoning confines of my parents' lives. I had been subjected to more of it than I ever cared to be. I never realized that it was a means for pleasure, because all it represented to me was pain and a secret that had torn me apart. The streets had given me a shocking education in the dangers of sex, too. I knew too many people who had gotten into trouble and ruined their lives because of it. It seemed too often to be a tool to obtain power or the admiration of others.

Having sex in this brazen and most unfeeling way promised to bring with it the kind of loneliness and emptiness I'd felt too many times before. I wasn't sure I was willing to risk not being able to swim out of a funk that would pull me down like quicksand.

I talked to Pop and asked him whether he thought that there was something wrong with me. For the first time in my life, someone explained to me about making love. He described the wonderful feelings he had when he held Mom close to him. It wasn't, he said disapprovingly, "getting in her pants" or "sinking his piece in her." He said that contrary to what many men believe, women weren't created to accommodate men's needs, and that making love to a woman was give-and-take, a mutual pleasing that was a product of love and affection built out of friendship. He said that if I expected to feel more than momentary satisfaction, I had to want more. That was what I wanted—to make love. I would rather have died than admit that around these guys. I maintained my privacy by acting like a quiet, mysterious, "don't ask me my business" type, while I did nothing to dispute their speculations.

I guess that was why I was flattered when

Kathy, who was thirteen and had a body that Pop called "jail bait," took a liking to me. She chose her clothing carefully to show off her maturing body. She hinted that she was waiting for the right person to go steady with.

"I hope the right person asks you," I'd respond blandly as my thoughts drifted to Janine, a girl with long blond hair whom I was in love with in the fourth grade. She was my friend and someone that I shared a great deal of myself with—or at least what I was able to share. It's funny, I never thought once of making out with her.

There was to be a dance at the firehouse for teenagers. I knew through the indiscreet and very tactless grapevine of kids that Kathy was dying for me to invite her. While parents talked incessantly about what fun this "teen jamboree" would be, I chuckled cynically under my breath because I knew that this seemingly innocent social event was a means to something that the adults either knew nothing about or ignored. The only thing on each kid's mind was the person that he or she would be making out with by the end of the evening.

Since I enjoyed the attention I got because Kathy liked me, I decided to ask her to the dance. She talked for an hour about what we would wear, who we would talk to, and even the way that we would walk in together. She even suggested that I spike my hair and that we wear matching outfits, but I said no to both. I didn't like to be crowded and this dance was already making me feel claustrophobic.

Mom bought me a pair of white pleated pants and a blue silk shirt, and Pop got me white canvas pointed-toed shoes that made noises every time I took a step. Mom got sentimental and took a roll of thirty-six pictures. Pop gave me his Polo cologne and fussed with my collar and the proper way that it should lie. He teased me about the goodnight kiss that I would steal. I wished that it were that simple. He pressed ten dollars into my palm as we headed out to the car; I asked what it was for.

"My son, my son," he said in a voice that immediately filled me with love for him, "you have to have money in your pocket when you're out with your woman."

"She's not my woman!" I declared adamantly.

Pop shrugged. "So keep it in case you want something to eat."

We smiled at each other and I threw my arms around his neck as he lifted me up. "I love you, Pop."

He pulled me closer to him. "I love you, too, son." Then he kissed my forehead and put me down. He glanced at his watch and said that we'd better get moving. I'll never forget the two of us, reeking of Polo, his arm around my shoulder and Mom walking alongside us snapping pictures as if this were a Hollywood photo shoot. I needed no photograph to capture that moment for me. It was great to have parents who cared enough to prepare me to go out into the world.

But from the minute Pop told Kathy and me to have a good time and left us off at the dance, I realized that this whole pretentious exhibition was not for me. From the get-go, distinctions were made between people who were considered cool and those who were regarded as nerds. Some black kids acted white, some white kids acted black. The key word here was *acting*, and I quickly became bored and impatient with it. One of Slick's friends said that all blacks looked like monkeys and asked me if I agreed. I told him that Pop was black, and I would check to see how many bananas he'd eaten that evening. Remembering the rumors about my insanity, he took off.

Five minutes into the dance I was sorry that Kathy was my date. In her effort to be cool, she was acting like a first-class slut, making suggestive gestures with her body to the song "Can't Touch This."

"That's a great song!" she exclaimed as she linked her arm with mine. "Hammer's a genius!"

"A real genius," I replied sarcastically as I removed her arm, "considering that he stole the song from a guy named Rick James."

"I heard someone say that. Is it true?" asked a frizzy-haired girl with pimples and thick eyeglasses who stood next to us.

I nodded. "My Pop has the record." Before I could go on to introduce myself, Kathy yanked my arm and told me not to talk to that girl because I might get some flying head lice. She made buzzing sounds until the other girl tore away. I stared at her in disgust.

"Why the hell did you do that?"

"Can't you tell? No one wants to talk to *her*." She said the word as if it were some dread disease.

I shook my head. "That really sucks."

A slow dance began. "Are we dancing or not?" she asked.

"No. Find someone who's okay to be seen with."

She did, too—without looking back to see if I cared.

I made my way over to the table where the frizzy-haired girl stood, and extended my right hand. "Hi, I'm Tony."

She shook my hand back rather suspiciously and told me her name was Patty.

"This is a nice party," she said, struggling for something to say.

"Actually, I think it sucks!" I responded. She smiled and agreed. It was the first time since I had been in Connecticut that I felt connected to anyone.

For the next hour, Patty and I talked without the phony banter, without the cat-and-mouse chase after sex. I bought us both a hot dog and a drink, and we sat outside at the picnic table next to a weeping willow tree that I'd been trying to write a poem about. I talked eagerly about myself, about Mom and Pop, about the books I liked and the songs I sang.

Patty talked about herself, too, stopping often to ask shyly, "Do you want to hear this?" I encouraged her to go on. Her parents had been through a divorce, and custody battles were getting her to the point where she stayed awake every night in fear that her father would steal her. We watched quietly as a few kids came out from the dance. Some were fighting and making lots of noise. Many were doing what they had set out to do in the first place—making out. Kathy noticed that I was sitting with Patty and gave me a "you've got to be kidding" look.

"My friend Patty and I are having a great time," I said, before she had a chance to make an unkind comment. She stalked away and I turned and smiled at Patty.

"Sorry about that," she said. I made a face and she smiled back.

It was Patty who broke the silence a few minutes later when she asked if a policeman's bullet had really caused my limp.

I chuckled. "You heard that, too."

"People don't talk to me," she stated evenly, "but I listen real good."

"I know you do."

We both became emotional for different reasons, so I did what I always do when I'm uncomfortable—I got silly. "So what do you say? Are you afraid of me or do you think I'm crazy?"

Patty studied me hard. "I don't think so." Her voice became gentler. "So why do you limp?"

I told her about the stroke and about how I woke up from a nap not being able to move the left side of my body. I told her how strange it felt to pinch my arm as hard as I could and not feel anything and to have to use my other hand to open my fingers. She was reassuring; she said she thought I was brave and that she was confident my leg would eventually move as well as my arm did. She told me she was glad I'd told her the truth, and that she was sorry it was necessary for others to make up such a story about it.

Rather than wait an extra hour for Pop, I offered to walk Patty home. I held her hand as we walked along in comfortable silence. I was relieved that the pressure was off to have to act a certain way.

"Nobody except you has talked to me since I've been here," she finally said.

That made me very sad. "You don't want to talk to these people, Patty. They'd ruin you."

"It might have been fun to have someone try."

"Don't believe it," I answered. I kissed her on the cheek and promised that we'd get together again.

I thought about Patty as I headed for the cabin and stood outside, looking through the window at Mom and Pop. "You Give Good Love" played on the stereo, the fireplace was lit, and they were dancing, their faces pressed together. Their expressions said that they were making love, so I sat underneath a tree and counted stars. I felt real and alive—sure that on that very evening I had taken the first steps. Pop was right about wanting more and being careful about not getting caught in the shuffle of quick sensations. I wasn't afraid. There were no more secrets, because sex and love and the decisions about both were within me. I was on my own journey, and this time my heart told me that it was right.

# To the Moon—
# No Gossamer Wings

The first realization I had about the seriousness of AIDS came on the night that Pop and I watched *Eddie Murphy Delirious*. Pop had borrowed the tape and talked Mom into letting me watch it with him. It was to be a special hangout night for us. My sisters were in bed, Mom was in the den, tunneling through piles of work on her desk, and we were ready for a great time. Pop threw some pillows on the couch, raided the kitchen for potato chips and chocolate-covered pretzels, and changed into sweats and a T-shirt. My enthusiasm built with the preparation. When we were situated, he popped the tape into the VCR. As the FBI issued the usual warning, Pop delivered his own: "Your mother isn't crazy about you seeing this because this guy has a mouth that needs cleaning out with lye soap and a wire brush—that's what I'll use on you if you repeat any of it." I nodded and we smiled.

We began laughing immediately. Mom walked

through a few times and made faces as she, too, cautioned me about the consequences of repeating any of "that trash." Then Murphy launched into his gay jokes, which quickly became AIDS jokes. Pop stopped laughing and a very disturbed look crossed his face.

"What's wrong, Pop?" I asked, puzzled by his abrupt change in mood. He looked stern and annoyed.

"That's not funny, son." He threw down a half-eaten pretzel and folded his arms across his chest.

"He's just goofing," I said, hoping to lighten things.

Pop just got angrier and gave me a sharp, disapproving glare. "You don't poke fun at misery, Tony—and that's misery!"

"Okay, Pop," I said, still not understanding. "I'm sorry." I was sorry, too. I just wanted to have a good time with Pop.

Pop put his arm around my shoulder as he shot dirty looks at Murphy. He told me how harsh and cruel a disease AIDS was. No one, he said, was moving fast enough to find a cure for it; thousands of people—good people—had already died from it, and thousands more were destined for the same. I knew a little about AIDS and even recalled seeing some horrifying pictures in newspapers and magazines, but I hadn't really paid attention because there were too many horrors in my own life and I didn't want to look at anything gruesome. How little I knew what lay ahead for me.

I never thought any more about that reaction of Pop's. It had passed, I imagined, like any other annoyance he'd verbalized. I remember it well now because I have AIDS, and the identical expression was on his face when he and Mom came into my hospital room to tell me. The words resounded in my head: "You don't poke fun at misery, Tony."

I had been through several batteries of tests. From the moment we returned from vacation, things had gone downhill. I kept thinking that I would shake whatever it was that was making me feel lousy. The only thing that anyone could tell Mom and Pop was that my lungs weren't working right. It could have been for any one of a dozen reasons. When I complained that I didn't want to have any more tests done, Pop assured me that they would be helpful because the doctors would know what medicine would best work for me. Again he said that we would "kick ass and take names," and that I would be better in no time. That was always how he got me when I threatened mutiny. He talked about that time in the near future when I would feel better and be able to do the things that I wanted to. After this day, however, Pop never asked me to fight again.

I was getting dressed when they came in. From bits and pieces of the conversations I'd eavesdropped on, I knew there was another infection in my lungs, and that they were sending me back home with some medication. Pop sat down on the bed and pulled me onto his lap the way that he always did. He wrapped his long, muscular arms around me in a gentle but firm embrace, rocking me for a moment as he bent down to kiss my head.

"My son, my son," he whispered as he held me for a moment in a tight squeeze. "You are one tough dude."

That's when my stomach sank. I was so familiar with Pop's moods, his choice of words, even his inflections. Mom smiled at me and then leaned down and tied a double knot in my sneaker laces. There was anguish in this moment—they had something terrible to tell me. More tests? More shots? Another procedure? I was sick of it all.

"Tony-Bob," Pop said as he shifted me on his leg so that he could look at me, "we've never lied to you." Mom smiled bravely again. "And we're not going to start doing it now." He kissed my forehead twice—his face tightening in such a way that I knew he was struggling to maintain composure. "There's a problem with your lungs—all the tests—the tubes down your throat—they wanted to see what was going on in there—your immune system isn't working the way it should."

"Sweetheart, you've got AIDS," Mom interrupted in her characteristically soft and even-tempered voice. Her eyes were filled with pain and fright. I felt sorry for her as Pop shot daggers at her with his eyes, almost as if to say they could have broken this news in an easier way. Maybe if she hadn't said the word, we could have skirted around the truth. Pop stroked the back of my head and pulled me to him once more as she continued, "There are things we're going to try to help you feel better—we need to take one day at a time and we'll work together."

Pop nodded in agreement. "We'll get through this, son." He didn't tell me this time, though, the way he always had when something difficult presented itself, that we would do what we had to do to make things better until we were shriveled-up old men.

Terrifying thoughts flooded my mind. I felt like a survivor on a lifeboat; I immediately started choosing those treasures that I could keep and those that I needed to fling overboard. I had stepped over the threshold between before and after. Marked changes were coming, the most devastating of them being that I had no future. I stared long and hard at these two people I loved so much. They were suffering. I didn't want to deal with them and their hurt, however. I knew what AIDS was—understood enough to know that I couldn't assure them that I'd fight so hard that it wouldn't kill me, because I knew that it would. I couldn't promise to go the distance as I had done before.

We all knew, as we stood around that room collecting magazines and stray baseball cards and deciding what to pick up for dinner, that our lives would be different from here on in. The focus would no longer be on working as aggressively as we could to seize life, but on resigning ourselves to accept death. No matter how many comforting words were spoken, how many hugs and kisses we exchanged, and how tightly we held one another, we were all lonely. A separation had occurred when we were forced to face the fact that our family would never be the same again.

I gave Pop a mock smile when he asked if I was all right. Who knew if I'd ever be all right again? He helped me on with my jacket and politely refused the wheelchair that the nurse offered. Then he picked me up in his arms and held me close to him again. He whispered something in my ear about a nurse that he thought that I had a crush on, and we both laughed. Thus the charade began as we both plugged our energy into keeping the other out of fear's way. We would fit the designated modes: Pop, the stalwart protector with the kick-ass attitude, Mom the soft and often subtle force who kept things in perspective for all of us. Me—I would just do what I could to see that they could follow through with their roles.

The certainty of AIDS integrated itself into my consciousness over the next couple of days. It didn't help that the movie *Longtime Companion* was on television the night that we got home from the hospital. The TV listings said that it

was about AIDS, and there were three stars next
to it. I was morbidly curious. It was a curiosity
that soon enough turned into terror. Bits and
pieces of the frightening reality of this disease
made their way through. The scene where the
man in the hospital bed is closed up on came
painfully close to what I imagined would happen
to me at the moment I was ready to die. I didn't
want to anticipate the terror and isolation, the
despair of my loved ones, the ostracism of those
who feared me. I shuddered at the despicable
thought of getting to the point where I would
need an oversized diaper and be spoon-fed or
talked to like a dimwit. How awful for such horror to be everyone's last memories of me. AIDS
doesn't understand that I've worked hard all my
life to be the person I am—the one that I want
people to see me as. I want to fall in love and
look into someone's eyes the way Pop looks into
Mom's. I want to worry about middle-age spread,
high cholesterol levels, and mortgage payments.
I want to see movies, read books, and grow from
one phase of maturity into another. I even want
to hate it sometimes. I want the luxury of being
able to complain about life because I'm cocky
enough to think that there's so much of it left
ahead of me.

I want things to remain ordinary, the way they
were just a few weeks before I was diagnosed,
on a rainy evening in August. Wind blew fero-
ciously, and thunder and lightning waged a
major war against each other. Pop and I hurried

around the house and shut windows as Mom busied herself putting snacks together to bring into the living room. We were going to watch a movie, since our original plan to drive to the shore was not very practical. Gina was collecting comforters and pillows and spreading them out on the couches. Robin followed Pop like a puppy, asking dumb questions: Could a window blow in? Could our house fly away? I enjoyed Pop's amused expression and admired his patience as he comforted her through her stream of what-ifs. Nothing was going on, but everything was.

As we gathered around the TV to watch *Dances with Wolves*, a tingling rushed over me—a sense of joy and wonder. My sisters fell asleep midway through the movie—Robin's head on Mom's lap, Gina's on Pop's left leg. I was positioned on his right one. The dog was asleep on his side in the corner, and the only sounds we could hear besides those from the movie were the rain beating against the window and the two girls' rhythmic breathing—a tangible and unmistakable sign of vitality. It felt as though we were immune to any harm or destruction. Right then, my family was pure and invincible. We were safe and far out of harm's way. Nothing bad could happen to us because we were surrounded by love. Pop gently picked up the girls and carried them to bed. I moved over when he came back, knowing well that he'd slide in next to Mom and that they would hold and stroke each other. This was all I ever wanted for all of us.

But AIDS was in our lives now, and it didn't seem as if we would ever be able to take comfort from a storm again. We would all suffer because of love—yes, even in spite of it.

Pop's gun was in its usual hiding place, so I waited until Mom was busy and brought it into my room. As I held it in my hand, I became frightened at its weight and coldness. TV never made guns seem this way. Pop sure knew how to handle them. So would I learn! I had been thinking about the book *Final Exit,* which teaches people about how to kill themselves. Jimmy Breslin had written a column about an AIDS casualty who chose suicide. It made sense to Breslin, and while he was sympathetic in all the right places, what came through to me was that he knew nothing more about AIDS than that grown people end up having to wear diapers. This sure is America—the only place I ever heard of where someone can make twenty bucks a pop teaching someone how to kill himself. Well, I thought about doing it, too—without the book.

Why, then, couldn't I stop crying? Why did I feel dirty and so cheated? Other kids were okay, going to school, having fun. They were only in bed to sleep. No one probed and poked their bodies. When they got sick, no one asked them what they'd done to get that way. Over the next several days, even the conversations I had began to change. Pop was no longer coaching me to "get on the good foot." He was talking instead about inner peace and not being afraid. He quoted verses from the Bible that spoke of eternity and how at the moment of a person's death he was never afraid, if in fact it was his time to "go to glory." We talked about the choice between burial and cremation. Besides planning for my death, I didn't know what to do, I had no control and no direction. I decided to get things over with and use the gun.

It was around that time that I became friends with the writer Paul Monette. I had read his book *Borrowed Time* in Connecticut. I wrote him a letter and told him that I thought he was terrific for not leaving his lover Roger's side when he became sick. We talked for the first time a few weeks after he received my letter, and we began talking often. It was he who told me, in an effort to comfort me on the day I was diagnosed with AIDS, that there was "loyalty among those who lived on the moon." If I had to be welcomed to such a frightening place, there was at least some comfort in knowing that I would be loved. Since he knew firsthand about the horror of AIDS, I told him about my plan, figuring that he understood the madness, positive that he would support my decision. At least now I had something to do—it was constructive and had a direction. I didn't expect him to disagree or to coax me into rethinking my position. He asked me to wait until morning. We talked for a while, our conversation centering on the here and now. He was excited about all that could be captured despite the specter that was imminent. I agreed to give things a chance.

A half hour later I handed the gun over to Mom, who accepted it, maintaining a cool and even demeanor. She took me in her arms and held me for a long time.

"You're alive now, Tony. That's what is, so that's what we'll do."

"What can we do?" I asked, feeling extremely defeated.

She kissed me and said, "We can live until we die."

The next day Pop told me that we would do whatever we needed to live for the moment. We had never given up before, and we were not about to start. He also told me that if I ever went near his gun again, AIDS wouldn't kill me because he would. He hugged me and said that he loved me, and I could sense his pain that for the first time accompanied his love.

I decided to try to believe again that wonderful things still could exist. I always need to say yes to life—even though it's tenuous. I will make it my biggest fight ever—because there is just no reason yet to say no. I'll stay on the moon with all of those who have been exiled there. I am in good company. I'll put in for a position as a star polisher; I hear that there are fringe benefits. You get to hear people's wishes—you get to re-member that hope doesn't die.

# The Body Mechanic

There's a whole lot to be said for being misunderstood. Those who are misunderstood are rarely seen for their true selves. Nine times out of ten they are either oblivious to others' thoughts of them or they flat-out don't care. I know one such individual. He has a voice that sounds like sandpaper rubbing against Formica. He rarely smiles. Those who are around him and who don't have some kind of history with him find him aloof, abrasive, and unfriendly. Not much of a conversationalist, he often gives one-word, monotone answers. He very seldom practices decorum, his grammar is scattered with *ain'ts*, and his English is rife with dropped "R"s and other characteristics of Brooklyn speech. Yes, he proudly states (as if we wouldn't know) that he is from Brooklyn. Ask him about Flatbush, Bed-Stuy, the old Dodgers, or Coney Island, and a strange and nostalgic smile will cross his lips. It's almost as if there were something magical there that belonged only to him.

At first glance, you might mistake him for a

Hell's Angel or a member of an old rock band. He wears jeans and T-shirts most of the time because he says that jackets and ties choke him. He rides a metallic blue Harley-Davidson and calls it his baby. It's not unusual to hear him speeding down the block at three in the morning, his black leather jacket flapping in the wind. You almost expect to hear a stereophonic blasting of "Born to Be Wild." But there is so much more to him—things that I realized only after spending time with him. For one thing, he is very respected by friends and colleagues. People pay attention to his thoughts and opinions. I learned from browsing through his high school yearbook that he was the class valedictorian. Mom told me that he was a champion baseball player and that he had won a chess tournament. One night when we were scanning with the remote to see if anything decent was on TV, we found *Citizen Kane*. He told me it was his favorite movie—always had been. He said, "Tone, we always go back to wanting the things that made us the happiest. They're usually something like a dirty sled, too."

He often overlooks when he needs a haircut or a shave, and his fingernails are usually bitten off—he can't be bothered with nail clippers or manicurists. Yet if you catch him on a night when he has to go to a formal dinner, you'll see that he can do a tuxedo justice—it actually looks like he wears one seven days a week—and he acts like the most polished gentleman who ever stepped out in New York. He's polite and charming, and it's very obvious that his manners are impeccable. Of course, he'll make faces and say that he hates every minute of it if you call him on it.

He has a whole list of things that he "don't do," as he so eloquently puts it. He "don't do sap" and he "don't do tears." He "don't do kitchen" and he "don't do kids." And he once declared adamantly that he "don't do Christmas." I respond to all of these things with a big smile and a hearty shrug. No, he won't cook a meal, but he'll spend twenty bucks on a grilled cheese sandwich if you want it, and then say that you had to eat something, after all. The kids that he supposedly "don't do" trail after him as if he were the Pied Piper—his explanation being that "they ain't got nothing better to do." The sap and tears that he vehemently objects to will always manage to tug at him—like a magnet to metal—and if you stick around long enough to notice, he is usually the one making the situation better. No doubt he'll say it's only because he "can't stand that kind of crap." Most of all, this guy who worked so hard at being Ebenezer Scrooge's right-hand man was the same one who snuck Kermit the Frog into my bed in the middle of the night. When I tried to thank him, he said, "I knew you liked that ugly bastard, so I figured what the hell." Yeah, right. He doesn't fool me, and whether he likes hearing it or not, he is one of the people I most admire. I see through those rough edges, beyond that perpetual frown. Underneath the hard exterior is a very gentle man whose heart breaks for every injustice that has ever occurred in this world. He would die before he would admit it, though.

We met when he became my doctor. A lifelong friend of Mom and her brothers, "Uncle Frank" was family. I'll never forget our first meeting. He walked into my room with a crash helmet in one hand and a slice of pizza in the other. I smiled and he said his usual "how ya doin' "—making it sound like one word. He sat down on the bed, offered me a bite of his pizza, and then began to talk to me about the football game on TV. The Giants were acting like a bunch of bums and maybe, he said, some little girls could teach them how to play. It wasn't until he began to talk about my lungs and other health issues that I realized he was a doctor—and a good one at that. It was very obvious that he knew what he was talking about.

He first befriended Uncle Mike at a party when they both battled for the attention of the same girl—a girl who turned out to be there with her very jealous boyfriend. I loved hearing about how the two of them had hid in the bathroom together until "Big Bad John" was out of sight. They began talking and realized that she had used the same come-on line with both of them. They laughed together, went to another party, and were best friends ever since. You wouldn't think they would have gotten so close because their personalities were so different. Uncle Mike was silly, always laughing and clowning around, and that's why my mom always called him an airhead. Quite the opposite, Frank didn't like scenes, and from what I understand, Uncle Mike got him into lots of predicaments. Frank said that Mike brought out the outrageous in him— and that "the bum needed someone to keep him out of trouble."

Frank downplays all of the wonderful things he does. There isn't anyone alive who is more difficult to compliment. He claims not to want to "hear nobody's problems," but if a crisis occurs, he is there no matter what excuse he gives. It was he who tracked Uncle Mike down at a work site to break the news that his mother had died. He didn't want him to get news like that in some cold, formal telephone call. It was pouring rain and Frank chased Uncle Mike as he screamed hysterically for three blocks down the parkway. As they darted in and out through traffic, Frank finally caught up with him and grabbed him. He held him for close to an hour as the two of them got drenched and cried. As Frank recounts it, "That crazy son of a bitch was gonna get run over—that's all we needed." He grieved for himself too, because Mike's mother was a sort of surrogate mother for him. Frank said that she was good to him, yelled at him when she thought he was messing up, gave him a shoulder to cry on when he needed it. She made him sleep on their couch so that she could make sure he was studying. During that time he kept a close watch on Mom, who was six months pregnant with Gina. He said it was because he was "in no mood to deliver no kid through all this commotion." The truth was that he knew Uncle Mike's concern about a miscarriage. He had already made it his business to keep that from happening. There was no doubt how much Frank loved Uncle Mike and his family. They had all been there for him when his seven-year-old son died of appendicitis. It was the combined efforts of Mom and Uncle Mike that kept Frank from killing himself. Whether he said so or not, Frank holds this family in his heart as much as he is in theirs.

It is Frank who tends to my family's injuries, colicky babies, flu symptoms, and other family ailments. It's obvious how much everyone relaxes when he is around. Whether he's placing a Band-Aid on a skinned knee, delivering a baby during a New Year's party, or opening up someone's chest to relieve pressure, he does it all with an ingenuous devotion that says clearly that he is a born physician. To him, it's not about a big bank account or extravagant vacations, but about the Hippocratic oath, which he is so proud of having sworn. He refers to it often, and it is as ingrained in him as his Italian heritage and his passions for food, football, and rock music. He knows his stuff, too. I have seen him go into a detailed explanation about the function of the respiratory system one minute, employing all of the ten-dollar words, but he is so unaffected by himself that the next minute he can call you a dirty bum for cheating him out of fifty cents in a poker game. He is offended by pain and is willing to kick death in the ass with all the street savvy that is in him—and it's that complicated and that simple. He calls himself a "body mechanic," claiming that his work is no different from a car mechanic's, except that his is done on human bodies. He resents the adulation given to doctors, because he feels that it belongs to medicine. Doctors, he says, are facilitators, just people who know where all the parts belong.

While we were all vacationing in Connecticut during the summer, this body mechanic showed his true colors more than once. A neighborhood boy cut his foot badly enough to need stitches. The logical move would have been to take him to the emergency room four blocks away. But his mother was hysterical—too hysterical to persuade to get into a car and do that. With his characteristic frown, mumbling expletives under his breath, Frank threw down the wrench he was using to work on his bike, and figured out the necessary treatment for the boy. He calmed down both the boy and his mother with the fewest possible words—the soothing effect of his voice is amazing. He refused to accept any money and went back to his bike as soon as he was done, making it difficult for them to thank him. When Uncle Sam told him that he had done a very good thing, he scowled and asked,

"Do you think I wanted to hear that woman losing her mind for the next three hours?" When he caught me smiling at him, he asked what the hell my problem was. Nothing, I responded, while inside myself I knew I wanted to be like him.

The following week, two elderly people who were staying three cottages away asked Frank to take a look at all the medications the old man had been taking. In his gruff manner he said he would when he got a chance—and made sure to do it that afternoon. I went with him. For nearly two hours he delicately explained to these frightened old people the course that a degenerative disease took, why each medication was essential, what part of the body each worked on, and the possible side effects. I could see the relief on their faces because they understood. He made them promise to call upon him if there were any more questions or if they needed his help, and he was visibly embarrassed when they tried to put money in his palm. Firmly he told them that he wouldn't accept it—that they were neighbors and he had already enjoyed a piece of her homemade apple pie. He even bent down and kissed the old woman's cheek with such tenderness that I wanted to hug him. I was so proud to be with him. I couldn't keep quiet when we left, and I told him that I admired how he had done such a nice thing.

"No, Tone," he answered. "It was the *right* thing!"

Of course! The right thing! What but the right thing? That simple principle escapes us all from time to time—those people who are put here to remind us of what's right come in all packages. Sometimes they even look like Frank.

He called his father "Papa," and had no qualms about hugging and kissing him in public. Whenever he talks about him, tribute pours from his voice. There was no one he loved or admired as much. When he was fourteen, he told his father that he wanted to be a doctor and not another partner with his uncles and cousins in their construction business. He received encouragement, and his father even set aside money every week to put him through college. During the last year of medical school, Frank's money ran out. He told his father that he would take a year off and work. Papa would not hear of it, and some hours later he gave Frank the money, saying that it was none of his business where it came from. Years later, Frank found out the money's source while making arrangements for his father's funeral. An embarrassed funeral director told Frank that his father's insurance policy was not valid, that it had been cashed. This was peculiar; his father was meticulous about always getting this payment in on time, because he said he didn't want collections being taken up to bury him. The date it was cashed, however, explained it all—Frank's last year of medical school. Not so strange after all. Frank reached into the breast pocket of his jacket and took out his checkbook. He signed a blank check and handed it to the mortician, telling him to take care of whatever his father would have wanted. Uncle Mike found him a few minutes later, crying inside a stall in the men's room.

"Mike," Frank said, "do you know what that crazy old man did?" And he told him.

"I guess he loved you, Frank," Mike replied.

Uncle Mike loved Frank too, and although Frank didn't say so, the feeling was mutual. Last year, when the news came at four in the morning that Uncle Mike had suffered a heart attack and died, I saw a very vulnerable side to this supposedly stoic individual. He immediately took charge and saw to the needs of Uncle Mike's wife and four sons. He took his place in line with the pallbearers and placed a strong arm around Uncle Bill's shoulder when he missed his footing. He looked after Mom and the rest of the family, attended to guests, and even washed dishes. When it was over and the people had gone home, he sat in the living room and put a videotape into the VCR. He ate a hero sandwich and guzzled a half-gallon of milk as he smiled and rolled his eyes at what was on the screen. He and Uncle Mike were playing football against Uncle Bill and Uncle Joe. He kept freezing the frame as Uncle Mike laughed out loud and exclaimed, "Frank, you're hopeless!" I watched for a long time as he kept rewinding and playing back certain parts of the tape—no doubt sifting through his memories and trying to lock them inside himself so that they wouldn't fade. No one who is as cold and aloof as Frank is often judged to be can know how to do that.

I'm glad that Frank is in the picture now that I have AIDS. I need his knowledge and his endurance and his absolute, vulgar honesty. He has no patience for sugar-coating, and he realizes well what an insult it is to do it. He tells me what's happening and then makes himself available for as long as I need to be coached through it. He, the same guy who avoids a compliment like a hornet and refuses to admit to a soft spot, is what he is. He can call himself a body mechanic, but everyone knows different.

So many times I have come close to dying, and Frank's expertise has saved me. It is his stubbornness, his commitment—even his cockiness—that buys me time. It is the compassion in his eyes when he says, "I'm sorry, Tone," that lets me know he *is* sorry and that he would do anything for me. If I die tomorrow, I will know that no one else could have kept me here longer. I've tried often to thank him, to hug him and tell him that I'm on to him. He'll either change the subject or walk away embarrassed. Every so often something slips through, though—like his outrage about AIDS or his anger at those who don't "do the right thing." It's obviously his credo—the only belief that enables him to live with himself. He's about down-to-earth honesty—the principle that governs him. It sets him apart from those who do a great deal of performing. No one who can sit and smile from ear to ear because he hears a song like "California Dreaming" on the radio can be as hard as he tries to make himself look. It's those little things that make him special. Don't tell him that, though. He'll just make an intolerant face and say he's just a body mechanic. Uh-huh.

# On the Way to the Mountain

For the last few months I've been watching the television series "I'll Fly Away." It takes place in the South during the early days of the Civil Rights movement, and the show usually focuses on the feelings and perceptions of the narrator, Lilly Harper, who talks about the changes she can feel. She is the maid of District Attorney Forrest Bedford. I use the word *maid* as opposed to the classier, more prestigious term *housekeeper*, because that is what she was called, and it is also the way she refers to herself. Her sense of importance always comes from within her—definitely not from the people around her. She is devalued by those same people because she is black—and therefore not worth the effort or attention to get to know. There isn't one time that she doesn't move me, that I don't come away thinking about something she has said. There did exist such harsh, cruel prejudices—and that bigoted frame of mind exists just as much today. Yes, people are more guarded about their attitudes, but those attitudes are still there and just as dangerous.

We like to pretend that we've come a long way—but it's not true. People still talk in derogatory terms about every ethnic group—as well as about fat people, little people, bald people, even stuttering people. Gay people are particular targets, and are constantly derided in the name of morals, religion, and sanity. It's easy to call David Duke a sleaze because he is a walking advertisement for bigotry. He's out in the open— we see him in action. But what we need to watch out for are the ones who come creeping around on sneaky feet.

Today they call crimes against people of race or orientation other than one's own "bias crimes." On the eve of Martin Luther King's birthday, news of a bias attack against two schoolchildren hit the front page of every metropolitan newspaper. It seems that two black children, eleven and nine, were on their way to school when two white children of about the same age caught up with them, sprayed them with white paint, and cut the girl's hair, taunting them with racial slurs while they did it. A couple of days later, a white teenaged girl was waiting for a bus when two black teenagers pulled her away and raped her. After the two incidents, leaders from both sides blamed the values of the other side. What ensued was an animosity that left room for future occurrences. The end result of it all is what occurred in Los Angeles. People begin to hurt one another without the slightest clue to why they are doing it. That city will take years to put itself back together. People everywhere are afraid to talk to one another or to experience others' differences.

My Pop is a big reason that I am sensitive toward such issues. David, too. David always told me that he felt as though he were in limbo—that he wasn't accepted by whites as white or by blacks as black. He called himself a mongrel—he thought he was being cute—but I knew him well, and what he was really doing was making a masterful attempt to hide his discomfort. That bothered me because I thought he was pretty great, that he had good looks, and I couldn't care less what shade his skin was. Other people did care, though, and he knew it. It broke his heart. He often said to me, "Tone, you don't understand, you've got the right looks." That felt so warped and so cheap—and I knew he was right.

Pop has never been bitter about his treatment by white people, but he does talk about difficulties that he has had being black. He mentioned only being able to go to the zoo on "colored day" as a child. He recalls harsh treatment in boot camp and various instances when he was not able to stay at hotels or eat in restaurants. He never held it against the white race, because he saw that as pointless. There were too many white people whom he cared about and who cared just the same for him. He blamed his bad treatment on ignorance and the inability of people to discard an age-old hatred, long outdated.

One summer afternoon, Mom, Pop, the girls, and I were driving home from the shore. We'd had a great day on the beach and the boardwalk. The girls had won stuffed animals, we ate so much we felt as though we were going to burst, and now we were singing ridiculous rhyming songs to pass the time. The car smelled of suntan lotion and salt water. Hints of a day on the beach were burned across our cheeks and our noses. We were just approaching the tollbooth for the turnpike and Pop said that we would be home soon. Then a police cruiser's siren ordered us to pull over. Visibly annoyed, Pop obeyed and stopped the car. Before he could even ask what the problem was, the cop ordered him in a nasty tone to get out of the vehicle. Pop did so and was asked for his license and registration. He was told not to try anything funny as he reached into his back pocket for his wallet.

"What is this all about?" Pop asked crossly.

"We'll ask the questions," the policeman responded in a hostile manner as he snatched Pop's wallet from his hand and began to go through the contents. "Where did you get this ID?"

"You've got a lot of nerve," Pop answered. "Where am I going to *get* identification like that? My picture's right on there."

"Are you telling me that you're an officer in

the military?" He asked that as if Pop had told him he had just returned from Mars.

Pop, who had no intention of going along or being intimidated, said, "It's right there in your hand. You know damn well that it's me. I want to know what your reason was for stopping me. What law did I break?"

"Oh, you know the law, do you?" I almost expected the jerk to start shooting at Pop's feet to make him dance.

Pop wasn't afraid. "You're damn right I know the law."

By this time Mom had gotten out of the car, and the girls and I were looking out the window. Pop told her to get back in when he saw the cop eyeing her with a disgusted expression. Keeping a proud and even grace, Pop stated that unless there was some reason for holding him—a reason the cop had better state in the next minute— then he was getting into his car and driving off. The policeman had different ideas. He warned Pop that he would find out immediately who the ID belonged to—that he might as well come clean.

I watched for the next several minutes as Pop was frisked, the car was searched with a flashlight, and very uncalled-for comments were made about the black race and about white people who made themselves trash by marrying into it. It was still not clear what Pop had been pulled over for, and although he maintained his composure, it seemed that any second he was going to fly off the handle and deck this guy. When the ID was verified, the policeman, not the least bit apologetic, said, "Well, I guess this *is* you. You can go." Pop grabbed his wallet and placed it in his back pocket, then turned to the cop and stated that he wanted his name and badge number. Obviously indignant, the cop asked why.

I was impressed at the way Pop replied, without raising his voice, "You've just treated me as though I was wanted in three states for bank robbery, and I *still* don't know why you pulled me over. Maybe your supervisor will."

"I don't think that's necessary," he said.

"And I don't care what you think is necessary!" Pop exploded finally. "You pulled me over and treated me like a goddamn criminal in front of my wife and kids, and I want to know what your basis was. I served this country for over twenty years, and it wasn't so that some young punk like you, who's still cutting himself on a razor, can fill the hours of his workday by harassing innocent people."

I was cheering for Pop—at that moment there wasn't anyone else in the world that I respected more. The policeman tiptoed around several excuses for about ten minutes, saying that maybe Pop was speeding or maybe he looked like someone else that the local police were trailing. "Yeah, I know," Pop said sarcastically, "we all look alike." He did get the cop's name and badge number, which he handed to Mom as he got back into the car.

For the next few minutes no one knew what to say, and Pop drove in silence. I tried to analyze the look on his face as he studied the road and looked several times in the rearview mirror.

After about thirty minutes, Pop broke the silence. "We've had a good day, let's keep it that way."

"Why did that policeman treat you so bad?" Gina asked. "You didn't do anything."

Pop obviously didn't want to go into the history of racism with an eight-year-old, so he smiled in a sort of sad but undefeated way. "He's not sure himself, baby."

We had a great time that day, but that whole travesty of justice never left my mind. If he could have gotten away with it, that cop would have beaten the hell out of Pop—I'm sure of it. The look of hatred was etched so clearly on his face that it had begun to reflect in mine and Mom's and the girls', too, a sort of poison that sparks an unstoppable chain reaction. Mom and Pop called it ignorance, and Mom even said that policemen see so much violence that they often don't know how to act or react.

I decided I didn't agree with that theory after seeing what happened last Christmas at midnight mass. Mom wanted to go—she said it was a beautiful service and it reminded her of her childhood—so we all got dressed up and headed for church. Fifteen minutes into the service, Gina became fidgety and complained that she was sleepy. Pop reached over, pulled her onto his lap, and cradled her against his chest. Within five minutes she was fast asleep. Pop kept stroking her head and rocking her gently. Gina looked more comfortable than a kitten in front of a fireplace.

That's when I noticed a woman in the pew behind us pointing to them. Throughout the rest of the mass she talked of how disgusting it was for that big black man to be touching that pretty little girl. I wanted so bad to turn around and to tell her to shut her trashy mouth. I wanted to remind her that she was in church—you know, that place where people gather in peace and brotherhood—but Pop would have been the first one to say that I was being disrespectful to an elder. This was supposed to be the holiest night of the year, the moment that began it all, but this woman couldn't see beyond her prejudice. All she saw was a black man holding a little white girl. She wasn't understanding the security and love that the two of them were feeling. It's kind of like when the judge asked me if I thought I would have problems coping with a black father. I laughed. I'd had a white father for eleven years and he nearly killed me. Wasn't that a problem to anyone?

There's a part in the middle of the mass where people are supposed to extend a sign of peace to one another. I turned and looked at that woman's face. She smiled weakly and I nodded. Still holding Gina tight against him, Pop turned around, smiled, and said, "Merry Christmas." I was so proud of him, and since we were in church, I prayed—prayed that his kind greeting would ruin her whole day. Even though it was Christmas, I didn't expect her—or anyone else, for that matter—to act any better; it's just that I thought it was a season when people should try to forget who they hated, if only temporarily. When the choir began to sing "O Holy Night," I thought of a story I had heard earlier that day about it. One Christmas Eve, during the war between France and Germany, a French soldier realized that it was midnight and got up and began to sing "O Holy Night." A German soldier heard him and answered with a German Christmas carol. For a few minutes, all anyone did was sing and experience reverence. I wasn't feeling anything like cheer or reverence sitting in this church pew as people shook hands with one another. On the contrary, what I felt was hatred and lots of anger, as I had that day on the turnpike.

To use such terms as "bias crimes" just means that we know how to label cruelty. I'm not very good at that kind of stuff—never have been. There was a problem one year—as there is every year—because gays were not permitted to march in the Saint Patrick's Day parade. This confused me, so I looked up the word *parade* in the dictionary. The definition said it was a public ceremony. What, then, was the problem? As far as I know, the public includes everyone. Someone needs to tell that to all those people in high places who have decided to alter the definition.

It's bigotry at its worst, practiced by those who conceal their true feelings with hypocritical words and smiles that would crack their faces. I don't think anyone told the Irish big shots, who were very choosy about their parade's attendants, that Saint Patrick—if you actually believe in saints and that stuff—was *Italian*.

I'm faced with a good deal of bias because of AIDS. People are afraid of me. They judge me before they even decide whether they can like me or not. I blame the ignorance of the present officeholders for that. During the presidential election, AIDS came up only tenuously in the candidates' campaign speeches. Why? Because it's a *biased* disease! Homosexuals get it, and it's their own fault. It's amazing how people rallied behind Magic Johnson when he revealed that he was HIV-positive. He was pictured on the cover of *TV Guide*, talking with kids about safe sex. There's nothing wrong with that, it's just that Gay Men's Health Crisis has been doing that for years. Of course, that group has the wrong name, so no one pays attention to them. If Magic Johnson had been wearing another set of clothes and not that Lakers uniform, no one would have paid any attention to him, either. He would have been just another black statistic. But he happens to be a famous athlete, so he receives countless awards. He receives applause as he sits across from Arsenio Hall and makes it clear that he definitely got HIV from a heterosexual encounter. If he winds up getting sick, he won't give a damn about how he got it. He won't think much about playing basketball, either. He'd better know that he is no more a man than any other just because he can shoot baskets and break records. My Pop always says that real men don't care about labels—that they just want to be men. They try to make every day count. They don't have to prove anything.

I harbor no animosity toward Magic Johnson; I hold it against those who have made him the patron saint of the nineties' curse. I feel for him now that fellow ballplayers are afraid of him. How dare they say that he is the first "mainstream" person to get HIV? What the hell is "mainstream"? What about me, and others like me? It's not going to matter if and when he gets so sick that he's just glad to be able to breathe or to hold food down or to hug someone and not have it hurt. Applause doesn't matter when you're wondering whether you'll make it through another holiday or another birthday, if you're lucky. Because it is looked at as a *behavioral affliction* of society, people whisper about AIDS *just* casually enough to make them seem intelligent while they're still able to maintain their distance or run away as fast as they can. Because, after so many years, it still takes someone like Magic Johnson to focus public awareness on AIDS, I'm not very optimistic about getting okay.

It really hurt my feelings when Dan Quayle said he hoped that a cure for AIDS was found before Magic Johnson got sick. Quayle is no better than those pretty-boy jocks who are so impressed with themselves when they can utter a complete sentence, but still I cried—from anger, I think. He made my sense of self-worth hover at zero! If the vice-president can express himself this way, from where can my sense of optimism come? He talked during the recent convention about family values. Who is he to decide which family has values and which doesn't? Because of people like him, I am not at all proud to be an American. It unnerves me that people must travel abroad to obtain drugs that might slow down the sand running through the hourglass. It bothers me greatly to know that those people who can't pay for medicine must go without it.

Nothing shocks me very much anymore, though. I was helping Gina with a social-studies assignment about the pioneers. The textbook casually mentioned how settlers came in and pushed the Shawnee Indians farther west until they were eventually asked to leave the state. That's the American way at its best—get rid of what's different, take what's not yours, and use force if you have to.

On the day of Magic Johnson's press conference, as people cried and responded with hugs and sympathy for him, Mom was sitting in the hospital awaiting some kind of encouraging news about me. There was no one from the press to hold her hand or tell her what a great job she was doing. When people cried because Johnson could no longer wear a Lakers uniform, Mom was crying because she wasn't sure whether she would be able to give me a birthday party. All of you who say you understand how badly AIDS devastates a family—you're talking through your hat unless you've done as my parents have and talked about living and dying with your child, the way you would discuss the next day's dinner. Until you have done that, you have no idea what it feels like to watch someone's heart break. I do.

We need to get away from labels—people's lives depend upon it. A crime is just a crime, an illness is only an illness. Antisocial behavior comes from within—not from skin color or the place where you live. If people could only set aside their prejudices and learn to care, I do believe we could find some solution. It really troubles me that I could have had a chance to live, but that I could die because of people's judgments about AIDS. I lie awake at night sometimes and stare at the ceiling, not knowing how to fight the rage. I think about midnight mass and a look of disgust during a moment of love. That mentality will sign lots of death certificates, including mine.

# Pork Chops

I've had to learn many things over the last few months—some things, as Mom often says, that a person my age has no business even observing. These things have been scary—downright terrifying and gruesome. It's not like those monster movies where you eat popcorn wide-eyed and wobbly and enjoy your fright. This is a fear that immerses you so that you can't keep your body from shaking. I've been fortunate enough during these times to have the right people around to see me through. They do more than their best, but when what you're hiding in the corners from is death, and you're alone in the dark fencing with thoughts of going to sleep or not, it's not that simple to keep from trembling. Since being diagnosed with AIDS, the prospect of my death has been a daily issue. I have had nightmares about lying in a closed coffin and looking up at the lid in terror as I try to convince everyone that I'm still alive. I pound on the lid and no one hears me, and I usually wake up screaming. Mom would often sit with me, reassuring me that this could not happen, but the fear was there and it came from the fact that I was not ready to confront what was.

Daddy and I watch "Murphy Brown" every Monday night. It's my way of keeping some kind of normalcy and routine in my life—and it's one of Daddy's favorite things to do after a long day at work. We like to watch things that will move us or at least make us laugh, and Murphy does that. In one episode, a dream sequence allowed Murphy and her best friend Frank to attend their own funerals. Dad and I had been on a roll with TV shows lately. Everything—even comedies— seemed to be about death. The episode was funny, although I could hear Dad bordering on hyperventilation because of the subject matter. Aside from the obvious sitcom laughs, this one was quite poignant and forced me to do a great deal of soul-searching. Although I laughed, part of me became afraid of Murphy and Frank's desperation to have some people grieve for them. I think people believe somehow that a true indication of being loved and missed comes from how much someone will actually feel because you are gone. On the one hand, you don't want people to cry and be miserable—but on the other, if you know they're too calm about your going, you can't help wondering what you've meant to them. Almost symbolically, Frank's urn crashes to the floor at the end of the service, and the funeral home attendant calmly takes a Dustbuster and vacuums him up. What a way to go, indeed!

That show left me frazzled. Of course I turned the issue around on myself and asked who I was and how significant I could be. *What* about Tony is so human that it wouldn't matter what happened to a bunch of ashes?

An old man who lived in a ground-floor apartment in my old apartment building came to mind. He had to be at least eighty-five. He had cornered the market on wrinkles, and there wasn't a tooth in his head. He smelled bad. Every day he would emerge from his apartment and sit on the front stoop of the building so he could say hello to everyone. He persisted, too, until whoever he addressed returned his greeting. Occasionally he walked up and down the block and whistled old tunes. The only one I ever recognized—and that was because I had heard it on "The Little Rascals"—was "Let Me Call You Sweetheart." (I almost expected to see Alfalfa turn the corner and start singing as the bubbles came out of his mouth.) In the summer he waited patiently for the ice cream truck to pass, so that he could get his vanilla cone and sit on the stoop with it for an hour, licking the sides and dripping ice cream all over himself. He always dug into it as if it were the first ice cream cone he had ever eaten. He talked for an hour after he was done about how great it had tasted. In the winter, he sat in the lobby with his beat-up gray overcoat and stocking cap. As people moved in and out of the building he'd smile and gum the words, "Real cold today." He made trips to the corner store to get his usual black coffee, one sugar. He read day-old newspapers and ate pepperoni sticks—amazing me each time that he could do that with no teeth.

Neighborhood kids were merciless to him. Sometimes they yelled obscenities at him, other times they bumped into him to try to trip him. He held his own, the taunts rolling off his back, except when they called him "Pork Chops." It was a name that sent him into a frenzy, chasing down the block after them. While I refused to join in with any of them, I admit that more than once I chuckled. It was the funniest sight I had ever seen.

"You son of a bitch!" he would scream after them. "That's not my name!" This only incited them to scream "Pork Chops!" louder. The harassment usually went on until an irate adult from the building would put a stop to it—at which point the old man would grasp the savior's arm and thank him or her a dozen times. "No problem," the person would assure him, and almost always rush to get away—no doubt to escape the offensive stench and perhaps the reminder that no one stays young forever.

One morning, as I waited in front of the building for David, the old man came down and took his place on the stoop. I nodded hello and smiled politely as he went on about how cold it was. Hector, a wiseguy from the third floor, came down and launched into his usual teasing, poking me with his books so that I would join him.

"Cut it out, Hector," I demanded, glaring at him.

"What's the matter, Tony? You defending your old man?"

"I'm not in the mood, Hector," I said with an expression indicating that I meant it.

Hector turned to the old man. "Guess what I'm having for dinner tonight?" Poking him in the ribs, he shouted, "Pork chops!"

Typically, the old man jumped from the stoop to chase after Hector, whose mother had just come into the building with a shopping cart filled with groceries. She alternated cross stares between the old man and her son. "What's going on?" she demanded.

The old man removed his stocking cap and said, "Good morning, ma'am."

She began to soften, her angry stares now aimed only at Hector. "Good morning," she replied gently.

"Would you do me a favor?" he asked her. "Would you tell him to call me John? My name is John Garibaldi—not 'Pork Chops.'"

She exchanged glances between the old man and her son. Then she reached out and grabbed Hector by the hair. "We're very sorry about this. That behavior isn't taught in my house." She tugged harder. "Apologize to the gentleman."

"I'm sorry," Hector said mechanically.

"I live in 3A," she told him. "You ring my bell if this ever happens again."

He bowed and thanked her, then offered to

carry her shopping cart up the steps. She refused graciously and made Hector do it, despite his protests about being late for school. I could see by her expression that she was as touched as I was. I was glad that Hector got his.

Two months later, John Garibaldi died. He was alone, slumped in a chair in his apartment. The super used his passkey and opened the apartment after realizing that he hadn't come out to sit on the stoop for a few days. Some tenants had begun to ask for him. After all, they said, he had no family and no one to see after him. That wasn't true, as I discovered when the super offered me ten bucks to clean out his apartment. The truth was that he had been married in 1927 and had six children: one daughter and five sons. He had thirty-three grandchildren, and one wall had frameless school snapshots taped all over it. He'd worked as a meatcutter, had been active in their union, and had retired at sixty-five. His wife had died of a heart attack in 1969, and shortly after that he'd suffered a small stroke. He'd rejected his children's suggestion that he go into a nursing home after getting out of the hospital.

On a wall that faced anyone entering the apartment were several awards and citations for exemplary work and volunteer services for charitable organizations. His name was written elegantly across each. I sat for a few moments among all these remnants of a long and obviously useful life. There were crystal and silver, a dozen suits in the closet. Robbers could have gotten in during the middle of the night and taken it all. The only thing that this man chose to defend with noise and dignity was his *name*.

I think about John Garibaldi a great deal now that I am forced to confront my own mortality. I have a very morbid curiosity about how the world will manage without me. I want to know what people will most remember about me. Will it be what I'd like them to remember—and will it be a memory strong enough to go beyond the fact that an urn filled with my ashes might spill and need to be vacuumed with a Dustbuster? Like old John Garibaldi, I want the mention of my name to indicate in a solid way that, for however short a time, Anthony Godby Johnson was here. I want my humanity and imperfections to come through. I'd like to know that I was a strand in this web of life.

Pop always says that we need to be very particular about what we sign our good names to. Whatever we sign must be worthy and make our signature look good. I understand. It's because our names are us. They are the foundations of what we are and always will be. There's no Dustbuster that can sweep that away.

# A Rock and a Hard Place

Throughout the many journeys I have made, there have been very few things that were secure. That was as much a given as Monday turning into Tuesday or night turning into day. The only thing in my life that was solid was David. He could have held many deserving titles, but when push came to shove, the words that would remain etched in stone for me were "best friend."

We have a rock in Central Park where our names are written in large block letters with an indelible black marker. About a foot away from that is a spot where we buried notes to each other that we planned to unearth in years ahead. They were messages that each of us designated for the other, and we would know where to look for them whenever the time came. We kept some of the dirt and put it in old spaghetti sauce jars. When we grew up and were successful with our "someday," we would exchange jars. Little rituals like these were the things that gave some semblance of normalcy to our lives. They said that no matter what, we were here, even between a rock and a hard place we were able to thrive and grow and know the value that the love of a friend could bring.

Sometimes when there was nothing to do and no place to go, we would walk for blocks, taking in the world around us. It was an adventure to brave rush hour at the Port Authority. We never saw the same situation and rarely the same people twice. We'd go down into the subway where the A train stops, and watch the variety of people who rushed back and forth. Everything was in fast motion. People dressed in suits, gripping briefcases and munching snacks bought from one of the dozens of vendors, looked nowhere or fixed their gazes on an evening newspaper, making disapproving faces at whatever they were reading. Some clutched at flowers underneath their arms and checked their wristwatches often. You could almost feel their exhaustion as they waited for the train to pull in. They knew that they wouldn't even be able to sit down for most of the ride home, but New York commuters are a resilient bunch. They do what they need to do—reluctantly—and then they go on to the next thing.

There was also that crowd of displaced people who used the Port Authority building as a stopping point to acquire some spare change or a bite to eat. David and I would have fun with their techniques as we tried to second-guess their next moves. Some panhandled, while others quoted the Scriptures. Some entertained. Cops were always charging into the bathrooms to get the drag queens to perform their floor show elsewhere. Nothing was as funny as watching someone trying to convince the counter person at one of the fast-food places to sell him or her twenty-five cents' worth of French fries or a dollar's worth of a hamburger.

Our favorite character was a large black man named Manny, who played the best rhythm-and-blues guitar I ever heard. As people pushed and shoved one another, Manny stood across from the token booth, away from the platform, playing his guitar and singing at the top of his lungs. Passersby flung change into his guitar case, and the more they did that, the louder he got. From Manny I heard the best versions of Sam Cooke, B. B. King, and Little Milton.

David thought that Manny was a step away from Bellevue. He argued that no one in his right mind would want to appeal to hostile rush-hour commuters. Manny never cared that they would knock him down or call him names. He preferred to pay attention to the bits and pieces of scattered smiles that made their way through all of the head-shaking. How could we draw that line between sane and insane? Were the people who stood waiting to spend their paychecks on the OTB lines any less crazy? It was all about survival and how good you hoped and wished that survival would be. So many things that were considered crazy years ago aren't thought of that way now, so maybe Manny knew something that we didn't. Despite the hectic pace, people *did* stop, even if it was to roll their eyes in amazement. They smiled and remembered when they first heard those tunes. They commented on how well Manny played. There was a peacefulness to his heartfelt crooning, and I remembered Mister Rogers again. His words need not only apply to small children. He said that just by being yourself you can make each day a special day. Manny was doing it, and I felt it. Whatever his reason, I smiled. Sometimes, standing on that platform with David and listening to Manny, I felt alive and part of something wonderful.

When I finally managed to get away from the nightmare of my first eleven years, I was able to look back and realize how fortunate I was to have met David. The close calls and the plain old ordinary times made the passage of each day smoother. Whether we were struggling through homework or looking for someplace to hang out, we did it together. That made life so much more bearable. My memories of him flood over me the way a cool wave does on a hot summer day. There are smiles that belong only to him—laughs that only he can feel as strongly as I can. There are tears too, tears that only David would understand.

It's funny how you never feel the impact of things until after they have long happened. To celebrate a friend's birthday, David and I joined a group in the school bathroom and swigged from quart bottles of Colt 45. We got drunk enough to be silly, but also to be serious. When I tell that story I refer to the way that we staggered to class and laughed our heads off as the teacher tried to get through a lecture on the Civil War. We were lucky because we could have been expelled if we were caught, but Mr. Blake just warned that whatever we found so amusing better not be so funny tomorrow. I rarely share the way that David, sitting next to me, three sheets to the wind, put his arm around my shoulder and said that if I weren't in his life, he might as well be dead. I was also bombed, so I giggled, stiffened up like a mummy, and said, "Start croaking."

He didn't want to play just then, and he said, "No, Tone, I mean it. You're the best friend I have. I wouldn't care about anything without you."

"Not even the Dallas Cowboys cheerleaders?"

He slapped my head. "Can't be serious with you."

I felt exactly the same way about him, and I should have been able to say that to him. He should not have had to be drunk to say what he did to me. But we didn't need to say the words. We *did* love each other. It wasn't a thing that either of us repeated with regularity—it just was.

I think of the fever of the *Challenger* flight. Enthusiasm buzzed around the fact that an ordinary, everyday schoolteacher was part of the crew. I wasn't impressed; I never got a charge out of anything to do with space travel. There was so much to the earth around me that I didn't want to go anywhere else. David said that he thought there might have been something to it because everything here was so messed up. I'll never forget coming back from lunch and sitting at my desk while the teacher talked about the course of history being changed. I half listened as he went on about the potential of space exploration. He said that perhaps in the next few years we would all be able to participate in some kind of space travel. I yawned and thought that this would be as good a time as any to nap.

Without warning, the spaceship exploded in the glory of its takeoff. I almost expected "Totally Hidden Video" to make their entrance, all silly and giggly. That didn't happen, though. The cameras continued to zoom in on the faces of the people as they stood there dumbfounded. They continued to replay it over and over, the fragments of the spaceship flying all around, and fire shooting in every direction. I became nauseous and was relieved that I'd never aspired toward the space program.

When we left school that day, I asked David if he still thought that space travel was a good idea. He shrugged. "I guess we're stuck on earth for a while," he answered. I wished at that moment there was a way I could make him really get it that we made our own trips to the moon by doing everything that we did here. I didn't, though. He would just have scowled at me and told me to stop reading all of those crazy books, because they were affecting my brain. I also was glad that he wanted to believe in something. There was a goal inside him, and even though it involved another galaxy, it meant that he hadn't closed off totally.

David took pleasure in a great many things that were important to me. I remember a baseball game that I played in, where I was having the best hitting streak ever. David was in the stands screaming my name and encouraging others to do the same. I went three for three, could have gone four for four if the disgruntled pitcher from the other team hadn't tried to decapitate me by beaning me with a spitball. I chuckle still, recalling how, just like Babe Ruth, I pointed to the left field bleachers to show my opponent where the ball would land. I was feeling my Cheerios and it got on his nerves, which is just what I wanted. I shook my butt from side to side and waited for the throw. He gave that pitch all he had—the spin on it catching me literally between the eyes and splitting my sunglasses down the middle. My legs gave out like Jell-O and I shouted obscenities and swore to kill that pitcher. I couldn't have killed a fly right then. I must have looked like the scarecrow from *The Wizard of Oz* as I got up and fell again. David yelled for me to stay put. I could hear the commotion as he got into a fight with that guy as the coach lifted me away from home plate. The coach took me to the emergency room, where they said my nose was broken. My heart was full and my spirit was in great shape. David was waiting outside with a proud but worried look on his face. He lied to the coach for me and said my parents were at work and that they were on their way home to take care of me. He insisted on accompanying me there. I smiled as our eyes met. His right cheek was swollen, his lower lip split down the middle. "We showed their asses, didn't we, Tone?" he said, and took a bottle of aspirin from his pocket. "You'll need these tonight."

We went to his house, where he took care of me all night. What could be more important than a friend like David, who would throw caution to the winds and fight your battles when you couldn't and then take the time to anticipate your needs? I was lucky! I know people twice and three times my age who have never felt so lucky.

Once, for an intercity speech contest, I chose Martin Luther King's "I Have a Dream," because I felt that it delivered the message of brotherhood in a strong way. David thought I was ridiculous and said that people wouldn't listen to me, just as they hadn't listened to King when he said those words more than twenty years before. Then a loud and obnoxious black activist saw the program and concluded that a white boy had no business reciting Dr. King's words. A boy named

Clifford, who was seventeen, black, and one of my opponents, told the activist that if he had any respect for what Dr. King had fought for so proudly, he wouldn't be insulting his memory with this bigoted attitude. He turned to me. "You give it all you got, little man."

David, who was standing on the sidelines, asked me if I still wanted to do this. I said that I did. He told me that he was convinced I had a grudge against myself, and motioned for me to follow him to the bathroom, where he had a white shirt and tie ready for me. He switched sneakers with me because his looked better, and took a blue cardigan sweater from his backpack. When I tried to thank him, he said I might as well look good while I made a fool of myself, and then told me offhandedly that I should do my best. We left the bathroom and he said that he would see me after the competition.

I was too short to reach the microphone, so Clifford found a milk crate backstage and instructed me to stand on it. "Give it to them," he encouraged me—and I did, even when the mike went dead, even when I caught sight of that angry man making faces at me. I won the contest, beating out some kids several years older than I—all of whom shook my hand and expressed hearty congratulations. Clifford had tears in his eyes as he said, "We're living the dream, little man."

Being in this contest among schoolkids of all races made me a participant in some small way in Dr. King's dream, where hopes become reality and compensation for all the other subsequent madness. For David to come and find me while other kids were being hugged and kissed by their parents said that we were as solid as any brotherhood quest that those before us desperately sought to create.

"You had to do it, didn't you?" He grinned. I nodded. "You did good," he said with the straightest of faces, "but you're no damn Martin Luther King. You got no rhythm." Whether or not I had rhythm, even if I was eccentric, David was there, willing to stand by my side and be who he was, knowing that whatever that was, it was all right with me too.

I guess that was why, three years later, I was thrilled when Mom called a friend of hers who was interested in taking in a foster child. He was a successful unmarried lawyer, and he had always said that he'd like to take a kid who was old enough to be self-sufficient but who would still need some supervision. This was perfect for David. His mother signed the consent forms without blinking, and soon David was living as good a life as I was. He had nice clothes, he and Steve (his foster father) went out to restaurants regularly—one of David's favorite things to do—and he didn't need to ride the trains anymore. While David was unwilling to consider this man his father as I did Pop, he did like him and admitted that he enjoyed being with him. I thought that everything was smooth sailing.

David was vacationing in Key West with Steve when I got the news that I had AIDS. When he returned and called with talk about deep-sea fishing and eating everything in sight during a buffet hour, he stopped abruptly in midsentence and asked, "What the hell is going on?"

"What the hell is going on with you?" I asked in the same suspicious tone.

"How come you sound so out of breath?"

"I got a cold."

His voice became softer. "You sick again, Tone?"

I sighed and blurted out the whole truth about the tests and the PCP. David listened quietly and took deep breaths. "Will you say something, David?" I said.

He was silent for a few more moments, and then he asked, "Do you still like the world, Tony?" I said that I did. "I'll never understand you," he replied.

We hung up the phone and I cried. I wanted to say so many things to him but couldn't find the words.

A few days later, Mom came into my room to tell me that David had died. He had free-based cocaine that was laced with strychnine and had a heart attack. He'd never made it to the hospital. For days I didn't talk about David, didn't think about him. Then I broke down one night and told Dad that I couldn't live in this world without David. I had never done it, and I didn't think it was possible. That was when he told me about Gary, his friend for thirty-five years. Dad said that he did his best to grieve for him because he didn't want it to be too painful to say his name or to recall those wonderful things about Gary that he loved so much. There were days when Dad had picked up the phone to call him and remembered that he couldn't. We talked until the sun came up about how it felt to lose your best friend.

There's always a story at the tip of my tongue and a lump in my throat when I think of David. I laugh at some things, get sad and wistful at others. I want to call David every time things get rough or when I get scared. I need his intolerant look to remind me that if we just take it easy, things will work themselves out. I remember the first time I saw David after I ran away. Mom brought him into my hospital room and left us alone together. He didn't say anything for a moment as he surveyed the equipment like the oxygen mask and the intravenous line. While I thought of something cheerful to say to him, David shook his head. "You look like hell, I guess you're going to die." We laughed so hard that Mom came in to see what was so funny. I learned later from Pop that David had left my room and cried like a baby.

These days I think more seriously about death and dying. I wonder if that's it—if, after you take your last breath, you are finished. Pop says absolutely not, Mom says that there is nothing stronger than someone's spirit. When David died, that was no consolation for me. Paul Monette asked me once if I'd ever thought I would actually outlive David. I didn't answer him, but when I thought about it later, the answer was yes. I don't think he was suicidal, but I also don't think he believed that anything could be wonderful for him. Denise sent me a letter that David had handed to her the night he died, with instructions to get it to me. It was days before I could open it.

*Dear Tony,*

*After we talked, I got mad about the way that our conversation ended. You and I are not supposed to get so mad at each other. You said that you loved me—I don't understand how you can find room to love anybody. I never did understand this about you, but that's why I wanted so much to be with you. You always laughed and you always cared, and I figured if you could, so could I. You believe in "wonderful," Tone. I always hoped that some of it would rub off on me.*

*I'm not surprised you have AIDS. I'm pissed at you for it, too. I hear you sucking in breaths and making real light of it. You've been sick for so long that you don't know anymore what it feels like not to be. That love stuff won't keep you here, you jerk-off—that's what I've always tried to tell you. You placed too much trust in that concept, and it never took care of you. If it would help now, I'd be a liar if I said that I didn't love you. Maybe that's why I'm so mad. I don't want*

*to go the rest of my life without you because
you're all I ever had to let me know that I wasn't
alone. Now what, Tone?*

*When I think of you, I think of so many differ-
ent things like riding trains and cruising girls—
sitting quietly and doing nothing. You made me
feel safe, Tone. You made the nightmares go away
because I was able to cash in on some of your
beliefs. Because of you, I believe that no matter
what happens, we'll be together. I don't want you
to be afraid and I'll try not to. You've got to know
that you are the best friend that I've ever had—
ever will have—and I'll be there if you need me.*

*David*

I have wanted to answer him. The first thing
I'd say is that love *did* take care of me; it took
care of David, too. He didn't realize how much
and how often we both proved that. I'd say that
he lessened *my* nightmares, that I was never
alone because of him. I, too, believe that we will
always be together—somewhere, somehow—and
that we'll be as happy as we looked in that old
photo taken a year or so after we first met. I
wish that I could hold him and tell him not to
be afraid. I close my eyes and see his face. I
hear his laugh. I smile at his scowl. David had
enough spirit in him for three lifetimes. That's
why everything made him so mad. What we had
between us had no ending.

It was meant that we would meet that day in
the schoolyard and that we wouldn't beat the

hell out of each other. It was inevitable that no matter how or why we were separated, we'd never lose touch. We are an extension of each other, and the distance is infinite. Love does that—whether we said it to each other or not. Unfortunately, sometimes it gives us pain and makes us cry. As Dad said, it's a tightrope that every conscious being must tread—and often enough it leaves us between a rock and a hard place.

# Cicely, Alaska; Hot Pretzels; and Purple Light

It is often said that the lights that shine through in the darkest moments are the most brilliant. I can testify to that, because there have been times when I have been sure I would never witness such beauty again. I did, though, in a variety of different ways, and each time I was grateful to know such majesty once more. There is nothing like opening your eyes after a long battle and realizing that you've made it through one more time, that you've tempted everyone and everything that said you couldn't. It's a bonus that you have emerged the better for it, knowing that you can wake up in someone's protective arms and experience the joy of seeing a familiar face or hearing a welcome voice. It verifies your endurance, especially when people are second-guessing your expectations for survival.

Such has been my case for the last several months. The onset of AIDS has brought complications I never could have prepared for. No amount of street savvy or previous experience with doctors, hospitals, and pain could lay the foundation for the long hours in bed, the countless fevers, the trips to the hospital, the intricate procedures, and the decisions about life and death. While most teenagers are discussing curfews or dating behavior with their parents, I'm talking about such things as not wanting to be placed on life-support machinery and my desire not to have a long, dragged-out funeral. I've discussed and planned with Pop about my cremation and with Dad about a memorial service. The hardest thing yet—I've asked Mom to let me die at home. It was heartbreaking to see the look of pain in her eyes when she agreed to it. Her pain comes not from fear but from sadness, because it is a request that she would prefer not to have to honor. When I gave Robin my bicycle, Mom said I had done a nice thing, but there was a hurt in her that went so deep that words couldn't explain it. She has been a soldier in this war that I live, and she is always ready to do battle, no matter what it might entail. If there ever has been a lady in my life whom I have loved and respected, it's Mom. When she smiles at me, I know that I have been very lucky. Hers has been an unconditional, selfless love that is willing to go through every day—ordinary or otherwise. I don't tell her often enough what she means to me. I know that I don't say "I love you" as much as I should.

From the time I received news of my diagnosis, there have been many changes in my life. One of the most difficult was when Pop was called away to a temporary military duty. These inconveniences are a way of life when you're a member of a military family, but they don't make us feel any better. To say that the house is virtually empty without him is an understatement. I always expect to look in the living room and see him sprawled on his favorite couch, engrossed in the newspaper or with something on television. I can hear the opening music of "Star Trek" and the clanking of ice cubes in his pint-sized metal stein. He takes it from room to room because he likes to have ice water on hand. I miss his boundless energy, his quiet patience, and I have longed for him to walk into my bedroom and say, "What's happening, Tony-Bob?"

I think of all the things I want to say to him; I remember the long hours that we spent together and the love that we built, one so powerful I feel it still. I hope to be able to tell him how I remember the two of us polishing off three ice-cream cones at a mall, knowing full well that Mom expected us for dinner in an hour. I want to thank him for telling me that I could do anything I wanted and that he would always be there to help me do it. I'd like to tell him I will always be grateful for that night a few years ago when he came into my life, latching himself onto me and not letting go, no matter how difficult things became. I giggle at how, when he introduced me as his son and people gave us peculiar looks, he would shrug and say matter-of-factly, "He looks just like his mama."

On a day when things get particularly hard, I close my eyes and hear him singing. I remember the gentle forcefulness that he applies to everything he does, whether it's playing baseball, doing his work, or talking about something he believes in. I think of his beloved copy of *The Velveteen Rabbit* and his emphatic declaration that love is the only thing that matters. I know that he's right. Because of that, I can keep in perspective who I am and set it apart from AIDS. This has been the time to remember the powerful words of "Invictus": "I am the master of my fate, I am the captain of my soul." They speak of choice and its power. They remind me that I am not the first person to have been cut down by adversity, nor will I be the last. Whether Pop is here or not, I will follow his lead and continue to kick ass and take names—and that is my choice, because I am an innocent man. Not innocent because I explain or apologize—but just because my situation is beyond my control. As he always says, "We're all going to die, so it's important that we make every moment count." It's not just a matter of being philosophical when we say that life is precious. It really *is*. Every time I eat something, I relish the taste and remember when I didn't get enough to eat.

I am the first to admit that the progression of this disease has not brought out the most flattering traits in my personality. I'm not always courageous or selfless, and being fourteen doesn't help. Sometimes I become moody and distant, sometimes downright nasty. Depending on how I feel, I can be a bad-ass who needs no one or a baby who needs everyone. There has been so much to be afraid of at such a rapid pace. I never did understand Roosevelt's declaration that there is nothing to fear but fear itself. That's been more than enough for me.

I've had so many infections and setbacks that I've lost count, and not a day goes by when I don't have an ache or a pain somewhere. I'm steady-dating an oxygen tank. Little by little I have lost parts of my left leg. First the knee went, then my toes, and finally the inevitable— amputation at the knee, because there were no more choices or reasons to save it. Those who love me said that it didn't matter, that I'm alive and that I'm still me. They have made courageous attempts to reassure me that being *me* is the most important thing. They're right, but there's nothing like suddenly not knowing how to put your pants on.

Often my trips to the hospital leave me feeling self-contempt. Doctors, nurses, and hospital staff are not always in the best of moods. There have been many times when I've wanted to bolt off a treatment table and to tell them to let me die. I noticed immediately that other people had "real diseases" that were no fault of their own. Theirs were afflictions that have made them unfortunate victims of nature. That has not always been the case for me. There's nothing like the look in people's eyes when they find out that you have AIDS. The first question they ask is "How did you get it?" and then they make judgments about how to treat you. I have had things yanked from my hands while being sharply scolded that I should watch what I touch. My possessions have been thrown in the trash because they have been "contaminated." Worst of all is when people talk about me as if I weren't there. It's as if I didn't matter or didn't have a mind. My feelings are immaterial, and my pain and tears are of no consequence. I suppose that's why an ill-tempered doctor said, oblivious of the fact that I could hear him, that working on me would be more productive on an autopsy table.

So much is said—and not said—about AIDS that it is no wonder there are such high levels of self-preservation. People don't know the right questions to ask—or even whether they should, in fact, ask questions. They aren't always sure they want to hear the answers.

There is a constant fear in our world of getting too close to anything, because if you do that, you might be more affected than you want to be. Still, AIDS always fascinates people. Every time we hear of a celebrity who died from it, there is either an insinuation that the person was infected by a blood transfusion or an obvious avoidance of that fact, an implication that the person was gay or a drug addict, in which case he got what he asked for.

A few years ago, when we read "The Death of Ivan Ilych," the teacher talked about the inability of the people around the dying man to acknowledge his impending death. Tolstoy referred to the "vital lie"—how in denying death people kept the horror of this man's disease far away from them. It made the dying man feel alone, afraid, and ashamed. Those feelings can kill you faster than any disease can. I see that happening all the time with AIDS, and it has to stop.

It amazed me that during the 1992 Republican convention, a big deal was made of the fact that Barbara Bush removed her red ribbon before she got up to speak. I realized then that politics was nothing more than a contest of ideas. The Democrats said the right words, like "gay" and "AIDS," and they talked about more programs for the poor. The Republicans talked about family values. I don't feel one way or another about either party. If I've learned anything, it's that we're all just people. Our values and beliefs are our own. No matter what we believe, we *all* suffer, we *all* hurt, and it isn't because of how we think or what we do, it's just because we're human. I don't think it made a difference whether or not Mrs. Bush wore her red ribbon; I'd just like to ask her why, if she thought to put it on in the first place, she needed to take it off. What would it have made her represent? I'd like to tell her that this is my biggest fight ever—that, like her sons, I would have liked to hit a baseball hard enough to break a window in my house. My family would have been thrilled to laugh and tell that story thirty years from now, but they won't. They'll talk instead of sadder things and harder times. I'd tell her that I'd considered writing the President and the heads of the AMA and the CDC, blasting them for not having done more. I doubt that it would do any good. I used to have this fantasy about chaining myself to the White House fence and making lots of racket. I wanted to be arrested and wind up in newspapers and magazines. But I realized that it would make news for a couple of days, and then just fade into the background like anything else that's too controversial. Silence does equal death, but there's nothing that can be done about that until the silence stops serving a purpose that frightens people more than death itself.

I will fight to keep a hold on who I am. I'll continue to assure people that they don't have to run away from me. My world is very small these days. Even some people who are steadfast in their fight against AIDS have fled. It's easier to think I'm okay and to tell people that. Often, for the sake of making things seem normal, I end up reassuring people. There is one individual who says wonderful things about me every chance he gets. He tells people that I am an "inspiration," and that I have made an impression in his life. He sure could have fooled me. He avoids having to say hello to me, and only does so when he's forced to, because he'd rather not confront me and see pain that might make him feel something he doesn't want to feel. I find his kind worse than those who are flat-out threatened by and appalled at AIDS, and show it. You know where you stand with them, and you realize that you can't control the way people think. When somebody acts like a fighter in the war, and then pushes away from the very cause that he's fighting for, he's a hypocrite and no better than the others. This person and others like him are the same people who will hear about my death and become outraged. They'll cry and tell my family how sorry they are—and they'll mean it! They'll go to protest rallies and use my name in their talks. I would rather that they tell *me* they feel this way. I've cried because people have not realized that even with AIDS I am still Tony, and that nothing can interfere with that. I like Whoopi Goldberg—especially when she plays a singing nun—and get hysterical at Bart Simpson and his attitude. I can cook pretty well, and I play a decent poker game. My favorite color is purple, and I love cats. I'm a lousy video game player but I can sing old songs and I've played Felix Unger and Nathan Detroit in school plays. I know Spanish curse words and enjoy showing them off. Sometimes I'm afraid of the dark.

Dad always tells people that he is HIV-positive. He thinks it is necessary to put a face to this disease, because most people assume that

AIDS is somewhere else. He tells whoever will listen that AIDS is a virus. It has no brain, no heart, no religion; it just goes where it can. It doesn't care whether you've been bad or good. "Some people," Dad says, "think that if they go to church on Sunday they're safe. But I've never seen a rubber church, and prayers can't stop AIDS, but rubbers can." That doesn't mean he doesn't believe in prayer, but there has been so much controversy surrounding the subject of condoms because people won't say the word.

Those who advocate abstinence are ignoring reality. The reality is that kids have sex. They're starting much younger than they were twenty years ago. I can remember classmates of mine doing it at ten years old. They weren't bad kids, either. They were good kids, studious ones with plans for the future. Some even went to church. It's just that there was this tool called sex, and rumor had it that it could open the door to love or power or closeness. Self-esteem is what needs to be addressed at great length, because a lack of it is usually the reason that kids engage in impulsive sex. Murphy Brown's out-of-wedlock baby doesn't mean squat. Talking about condoms and birth control would probably do lots of kids a favor. At the very least, it would provide an option. From where I sit, I think that *anything* that will prevent this nightmare from happening even to one other person should be talked about. Pop says that God helps those who help themselves. That message is what needs to sink in so that someday we won't have a disease like AIDS that we need to put a face on.

I had a fellow patient named Barry, who rambled on often about his disappointment with life and people. He was rude to everyone—feeling that he was justified because he was sick and everyone else wasn't. Everything that happened to him was always someone else's fault. He should have had Pop around to inform him that if he didn't cut the crap, he would be a lot sicker real soon.

While talking about how horrible the world was, Barry pulled out his copy of *Final Exit*. He pointed to chapters that spoke boldly of suicide. Barry reasoned that I would be doing my loved ones a favor by sparing them the misery of witnessing my death. He called it a man's way out. Though I tuned him out, I wondered how true any of his rambling was. I was sick so often that the tense and worried looks on people's faces were not getting past me. The nights were getting longer, and the spaces in between where things should have been all right seemed fewer. Every time I underwent some procedure, I studied people's reactions to what they were doing. No one ever smiled. They shrugged an awful lot. More than once I heard mixed exasperated comments about some procedure being futile or a waste of time. I began to question the reason for any of it. Why struggle so hard? Why cooperate? Why bother to endure?

Then I remembered Dad and me pulling on

long johns, boots, and parkas and heading for Cicely, Alaska—the locale of the TV series "Northern Exposure." On my fourteenth birthday he snuck me a beer while we lunched at Holling's place. We stopped at Ruth Anne's store for cherry Popsicles and walked hand in hand down the street, searching for the moose in the opening credits.

We go to the lake and sit on our favorite log. We hold each other, and his arms feel good around me. I might recite Frost's "Stopping by Woods on a Snowy Evening." We gave each other Indian names. He named me He Who Sees Clearly with Heart. I called him He Who Holds with Firm Grips. It's an appropriate name for him, because I lose my grip from time to time, and he is there to supply it for me. These times know no circumstances and have no concept of the hour. They happen when I need to cry but don't want anyone to be afraid of my tears. They come in the middle of the night, when I wake up and feel as though I'll die. That imaginary hourglass uses pain and discomfort to taunt and remind me that this is the worst nightmare that can happen to anyone. Dad willingly lessens its burdens and points me in the direction of dreams more worthy of my investment.

Our times in Cicely are precious and meaningful. They are wonderful enough to override the fact that these are journeys we take only in our minds. It is a game that succeeds for a while in keeping the ugly reality away. It doesn't matter if I'm lying in bed hooked up to oxygen because it is so hard to breathe. We're together and we're making our own fun. Miserable people like Barry and skeptical doctors who get annoyed because we don't adhere to their schedules—when we are born and when we die—don't know about Dad's power to relay how much more the quality of our time matters than its quantity. He can't change what is—doesn't imply for a minute that he can—but he works wonders with what we have. We take our existing situations and turn them into the biggest possible parties. He never runs away from what is painful; he's just genuinely sorry about it. He understands loneliness and knows how important it is to be a person with a first name. When he's scared, he says so. It's okay that I hear him cry or that I know when he's not feeling strong. We don't have to follow an agenda or a format. I know that when he said he'd signed on for the ride—however bumpy—he meant it. We've had smooth times too, though. Last Christmas he and I were like two mice, opening our gifts at one-thirty in the morning. We squealed and giggled; whoever might have eavesdropped would have thought we were as normal as any other dad and his son.

He knows me well. He anticipates those times when I explode in anger. He can interpret my painful silences. It is he who will wake up out of a sound sleep and sing "Mood Indigo" to quiet the pain that makes me want to quit. His voice has an extremely calming effect on me. Dad has taken away my should-haves and taught me that *right now* is my most valuable resource. I am at peace with the fact that I am a magician creating my own present. I know that the sun rises even if I don't wake up to see it. I'm betting that someday Kermit the Frog will find his Rainbow Connection; Dad has pushed the rain to the side and seen to it that I have finally found mine.

He cried with me when I told him how surviving among those callous health-care workers is harder than getting through a gang war in Harlem. I watched a man die while waiting for a procedure to be done at the hospital. I didn't know his name, he was just a man on the moon who had the misfortune of being at the mercy of insensitive people. My heart broke for him as if he were a lifelong friend. I tried to talk to him, struggled to find the most comforting words, thanked God that it wasn't me feeling the desperation. He pleaded for someone to give him something for his pain. They dismissed him impatiently and told him to be still and wait until his procedure was done. He gasped and sweated for what seemed close to an hour. Finally, when it was too late, a few nurses and a house doctor hovered over him and announced that he was dead. They made comments about how merciful it was—the doctor was glad that the "poor slob" was out of his misery.

No one held his hand or made any kind of gesture that showed sorrow for the loss of a human life. No one said "I love you," or told him he shouldn't be afraid. I've seen more compassion aimed at a dog lying in the gutter in the ghetto. I cried later that night for him—and for myself—and for every other man and woman on the moon who is forced to know that iron-handed disregard.

I asked Dad please not to let me die at that hospital, alone with those inhumane people. It would make me feel that all the life I clung to was of no value. He promised that I wouldn't—swore that I wouldn't be afraid because he wouldn't let it happen. Then he did a couple of things. He told me that he loved me and he sent me pretzels—you know, the ones they sell on pushcarts outside of the bus terminal at Times Square. David and I were more than thrilled whenever we could scrape up a buck and a quarter to get one. We always knew where to find the vendors because they were identifiable by the sharp aroma of charcoal that socks you in the face. When I bit into the pretzel that Dad sent, Times Square and its hustle came back. So did David, and Manny and his guitar. Daddy understands that some parts of yesterday are sweet and worth reliving. They reaffirm with a passion that we're here in spite of—or because of—those who don't comprehend that we haven't chosen to die yet. Because he knows that wounds can go deeper than words can say, he sees to it that the horrid taste of dispassionate, unthinking medical assembly line workers leaves my mouth so that I can make room for the rich taste of charcoal and hot pretzels and the magic that they bring. No one can taste that splendor and be on an autopsy table at the same time. There is no futility in savoring every bite of something wonderful.

Dad has also created a purple light for me. It's perpetual, present whenever my spirits are low and I feel hopeless. He assures me that it will wash over me and bring courage and protection. He guarantees that it will make my journey from this world into the next a good one. It supplies the passion I need to face AIDS and to fight it. This wonderful light can help me combat a fever, the pain of isolation and rejection, and my fear of dying. It says that I will never be alone. It says that Dad and his purple light will be there to shine love on me, making mine an exodus of glory.

There is no doubt that I will die soon. I know that well—my body is a constant reminder of that fact. I'll have to forgo those plans for a career in major-league baseball. There will be no five-o'clock shadow sprouting on my face, my voice will never lower to that bass tone I have anticipated all of my life. I'll never be able to abuse credit cards or balance my checkbook. Falling in love and making out with the girl of my dreams will have to remain a fantasy in my heart. That's not so bad, I tell myself, because I can pick the time, the place, and the girl, and it will always be wonderful. I'll never know the disillusionment that comes sometimes with maturity, experience, or bad timing. I convince myself that I won't have to suffer the throes of rejection because it's much easier than thinking that I've lost out or am missing something.

I often wonder about the last moment on this earth for me. My successes and failures can only be gauged on a small scale of incidental occurrences. My ego and just plain human nature make me want to contribute to society and the world at large in some marked and crucial way. I'd like to know that people won't forget me, that when all is said and done, it won't matter that my time was short. I'm here—have been here—for however short a time, but I have moved civilization for just being me. I no longer believe that I am an accident of birth, and have long dismissed the thought that I am an irrelevant human being who is unable to touch those around me. I am not an object of shame, but a portrait of pride. I hold my head high and say my name aloud.

Every night, around midnight, I hear the grate go up as the saloon down the street opens. A short while after that, garbage trucks pass, making lots of noise. You have to be in a deep sleep not to hear them, and I almost always do. At around three in the morning the grate comes down again, and it signals to me that the night is just about over; I feel as though I have tempted fate and made it through another day. No matter how horribly things are going or how sick I feel, the rickety sound of that grate tells me that I am still alive. Again.

At the moment of my death, I want three things. I want not to be afraid. I want the people

I love to know just how much I love them, and that a part of me will be inside them and make them smile every time they think about me. For someone who spent a great many years thinking that nothing good could come to me, I'm doing quite well. Though I thought I would never rid myself of my aversion to the word *father,* I have found two who are unsurpassed. I want them, as well as Mom, to know that what is in our hearts will always be there. Most important, I want to know that I have done everything that was humanly possible to contribute to my world in some kind of way. I want to give back in gratitude for having been able to be here. I hope that this story of a life well lived can be my contribution.

Dad's purple light shines on me—and will do so even when I'm gone. It will forever reflect on him; our love will see to that. We will persevere to chip away at those who remain locked in fear, intolerance, and indifference. We do so with love while we ask for indulgence. We beg for a civilized and constructive meeting of minds, devoid of judgments and free of recriminations. We will continue to embrace—and overcome—all of those who have forgotten that we *are* our brothers' keepers, and neither the Bible nor religion has a thing to do with it. We need to fight for this ideal with all we have. Everyone's life depends upon that. I do it in Cicely, Alaska. The weapons that I choose: hot pretzels and purple light.

—Anthony Godby Johnson
1992

# Epilogue
## And Then ...

There is nothing like an AIDS diagnosis to detour the course that a person has charted for himself. Mine forced me to look at what my life had meant and what it would come to represent—for me and the people I loved. I had to keep a hostile respect for the hourglass and at the same time figure out what I would choose to do with the rest of my life. Baseball became a game that I loved but could only watch, and *A Rock and a Hard Place* became one of my most rewarding compromises.

At age fourteen most people don't get philosophical about wanting to leave a mark. There's still too much living left; a few more decades, several more stories, crow's feet, and mistakes made that leave a wistfulness about doing and not doing things—all that would make for a good memoir. However, knowing that your time is limited is the best incentive to reminisce. Things can't help but become poignant, and memories have no choice but to be sweeter when you're fighting to hold onto them. There's that longing inside you to experience them again, that wish you could make time stand still so you could have one more chance to appreciate your life for what it's really worth. I have come to understand that things change so continually that even when something is horrible, it probably will not stay that way. In finally letting go and learning that fact, I became reflective and felt the need to write things down, to recall, to sift through incidents that taught me things and that brought who Anthony Godby Johnson was into a clearer, more detailed focus.

My pop says that the lessons we learn are what make us who we are. So I looked back to the strongest ones, the most indelible impressions, and chose the subjects for the essays that make up *A Rock and a Hard Place*. As I worked on them, these essays became what I think is the most honest portrayal of how as I see myself and how I imagine others see me, too.

I've just turned sixteen, AIDS is still my bitterest enemy, but I believe it has come to know that I will fight it back with everything I have. I have had no choice but to become mature in ways that are, perhaps, uncommon for kids my age. I neither lament this, nor do I celebrate it. There is nothing to celebrate about a life that is cut short. On the other hand, there are causes for celebration when you make the decision to live life on a day-by-day basis.

Yes, I love being my age and saying that I wrote a book. But more than that, I love knowing that I did have a say in the world, that my thoughts were considered, if just for a little while, by people I don't even know about. A reporter tried to discredit me by theorizing that I didn't exist and insinuating that someone my age could not write my book. I was so hurt that I wanted to give up. It was my faith in the people who I love—and who love me—that prevented me from deciding it was time to die. I won't go into what the reporter said and what was not true about it, but I will say it is a shame that a child can still be silenced or made to regret having the courage to tell a difficult truth. When this happened to me, I spent night after night wanting to slap myself for telling the secret— that those adults were right and I was wrong. I thought back to those nightmarish times and remembered being told that no one would ever believe me. The truth was, as my new dad pointed out, that people ultimately believe me. People *were* on my side, and they were offended at the thought that someone *wouldn't* believe me.

We could populate a country with people who have stories similar to my own. Children are basically powerless beings who have to trust in their parents' mercy. But that's why Lisa Steinberg died as well as many other unpublicized children who lived the same nightmare. That's why a child can be taken away screaming from the arms of her adoptive parents and given to the biological parents who gave her up. That's why Kimberly Mays and Sean Russ had to go to court and create a stir. That's why I have AIDS. No adult was around to act on our behalf until it was too late and the damage was already done. In our cases there had to be an uproar before those who could do something finally did.

Unfortunately, until people stop turning away, until children can confidently look up to adults and rely upon them for help, my story will remain just one of many. People will read about us, shake their heads for a few moments, and still ignore us. As much as they delude themselves into believing that the system is set up to protect children, it isn't true. There are too many kids, too many technicalities, special cases, and loopholes, and the truth is, what's bad is bigger than we are.

A reporter questioned my ability to write, wondered how I knew things that were way beyond my years. As my friend Jose Perez told me, "When things like this happen to you, you're no longer a child." There is a tug-of-war between the world that you chronologically belong in and the one that you are actually a part of. Jose, a successful adult today, recently decided to visit the place where he had been abused some twenty-five years ago. He saw the window he was pushed through because he didn't get the hang of riding a bike. He looked into the room where he received a beating that landed him in intensive care for a month. He talks about how in this very place he grew old and missed his childhood. I never thought that I was a child either. To be a child you must trust in the adults around you, and I couldn't. It is only since I've been with my mom and pop that I have learned to play games—and feel good about it. It has only been here that I have understood what it means to have fun, to relax, to have a full stomach and to sleep peacefully.

There are still those parts of me that are very old—locked away and damaged beyond repair. No one can retrieve those parts but me. They resurface from time to time to remind me that I have been hurt. Writing helps me during those times because while I was never permitted to speak out for myself, no one ever had any control over what I put down on paper. It was always my way of silently screaming. It was a way for me to communicate, if only with myself. As long as I could wield a pen, I was bolder, freer, and that much more honest. No one was turning around to look at me, and I wasn't ridiculed.

I learned by reading other people's works that there was something to a point of view—that there were many to choose from and that mine was unique and worth developing. When I began to reveal who Tony was, I thought once again of E. B. White's comment, "Writing is both mask and unveiling." While I knew I wanted to say a great many things, there were other things that I was unwilling to talk about—things that are locked in the corners of my mind and accessible to no one.

*A Rock and a Hard Place* began as a means of sorting and regrouping those and other things and finally turned into a picture of me. Rereading it over the last few months, I was able to understand better why I did some of the things that I did, why it was impossible for my life to happen any other way. That knowledge has helped me to reconcile myself to those errors I was sure I made and those shortcomings I was positive I had. I am at peace knowing I did the best that I could. Sure, the demons of yesterday crop up sometimes and make me think that I am not free, but with the love and patience of those around me, I am able to resist and to turn them away.

The fact that I can write is due to the teachers who emphasized the power of the written word and the importance of mastering the English language. It's a sorry statement on this country's education system that people were so skeptical that someone my age could write a sentence. Yes, I can write. I've also read more books than a lot of people three times my age, I've memorized poems and speeches, and I know songs that are older than my parents. I can read music and I can draw. I also know how to use a gun, pop a switchblade, hot-wire a car, and hold my own in a fistfight. I still am fascinated when I learn something new, and I have just finished reading a collection of "little golden books" that belonged to my sisters. I never got to enjoy them before, so I'm doing it now. A reporter who has not taken the time to get to know the many sides of a person has no right to draw conclusions. I've learned, though, that all is fair in tabloids and war. Most important, I've learned that when something is inaccurate or insignificant, you either correct it or leave it alone.

The people who have read and responded to my book have brought me a lot of joy. Irvin Sasski, a schoolteacher in Hawaii, introduced me to the beautiful island that I will never be able to visit. Jim Knoll came from Atlanta to bring with him the AIDS awareness play *Straight from the Heart,* meringue balls, and a bubble gun. He takes advantage of modern technology by sending me faxes that say "good morning," "have a good day" or "I love you". Don Hickenbottom in Washington sends memorabilia about his state, long handwritten letters about his childhood and his three jobs, along with copies of his high school yearbook from 1940. Mauricia Stadey in Oregon calls herself my "number one groupie" and Tammy Lacher tells me about the beautiful mountains in Colorado. There's Mary Jo in Washington, Pennsylvania. We talk about zapping the narrow-minded, changing the world, and enjoying delicious food while we do it. Her eighty-year-old son, Nathan, has introduced me to the wonderful world of SEGA video games, and her girls Amy and Lisa keep me informed about the goings-on of the adolescent world.

Grandmothers have baked me cookies, a song was written for me, and I've received baseball caps, coloring books, and kind words from mothers who have told me that they will hug their kids a little more. People send prayer wishes, and a judo instructor sent me a black belt. A woman on welfare wanted me to know that she would not give up on her own life because knowing about mine had given her hope. Her four-year-old son draws me pictures. A seventeen-year-old girl wrote to tell me that after reading the book she decided against suicide.

I still believe in love, and no, I'm not a Pollyanna. Dad and I still go after that purple light to get us through the rough moments. We still watch *Murphy Brown* and *Northern Exposure,* and he still buys me enough junk food to feed an army. My body mechanic still feigns indifference to what he cares about, my pop still kicks ass and takes names, and my mother has not wavered. She is the sunshine during the darkest moments, the tower of strength when everyone has had it.

AIDS and its effects are still with me too. There is nothing I can do to change that. I'm here, though, and that stands for a great deal. I chose not to be public as the AIDS poster child because something told me that the focus would go off the disease and onto me—emphasizing in people's minds that this disease deserves attention only if the person who has it is by their definition, innocent. I'm not a hemophiliac, nor was I an IV drug user. I'm not gay either, but many of my very good friends are and I defend their right to celebrate that fact. Readers of *A Rock and a Hard Place* will miss the point if they extend all their sympathy in my direction. I am not in this situation because I was innocent and got caught by a behavioral disease, but because I was innocent and unprotected in a society that is too busy with labels and innuendo.

If I had given up, I would have missed out on many things that I would never have imagined could happen to me. I have had the privilege of falling in love with a girl named Jennie, and while things can't be the way that we want, we are living in today. Not even AIDS can take away what we have. I would not have met the good friends that I have—friends who have been mainstays for me. During those times when things looked hopeless, I never imagined Armistead Maupin and I could joke about a funeral or that Darryl Ponicsan would teach me the Hollywood particulars of deciding who buys lunch.

Yes, sometimes life leaves you between *A Rock and a Hard Place*. But as many people have made the effort to show me, flowers grow in between them, and they are beautiful.

# *Afterword*

Once in a great while a child comes along whose understanding of eternal truths has a way of encouraging adults to stop and wonder. Tony Godby Johnson is such a child. Despite all of the horrendous difficulties of his young life, Tony emerges as a teenager whose innate wisdom can enlighten the most learned sage.

When I once told Tony that someone had asked me if we ever dealt with AIDS on our preschool "Neighborhood" television program, Tony's reply was, "I don't think it has a place there, Mister Rogers. Keep the Neighborhood innocent. Kids need a quiet place with subtle and loving messages that allow them to know what CAN BE."

Tony's story is a testimony to what CAN BE even against the most defeating odds. It speaks to the life-giving difference that unselfish love can make when someone is caught in that space between a rock and a hard place.

Tony's softening of that space in his life gives hope to all of us.

—*Fred Rogers*